CULTURE SMART!

HONG KONG

Clare Vickers and Vickie Chan

·K·U·P·E·R·A·R·D·

This book is available for special discounts for bulk purchases for sales promotions or premiums. Special editions, including personalized covers, excerpts of existing books, and corporate imprints, can be created in large quantities for special needs.

For more information contact Kuperard publishers at the address below.

ISBN 978 1 85733 869 0

British Library Cataloguing in Publication Data
A CIP catalogue entry for this book is available from the British Library

First published in Great Britain
by Kuperard, an imprint of Bravo Ltd
59 Hutton Grove, London N12 8DS
Tel: +44 (0) 20 8446 2440   Fax: +44 (0) 20 8446 2441
www.culturesmart.co.uk
Inquiries: sales@kuperard.co.uk

Series Editor Geoffrey Chesler
Design Bobby Birchall

Printed in Malaysia

About the Author

CLARE VICKERS is an English writer who lived in Hong Kong for eighteen years. Her husband was a member of the Hong Kong government until 1997, and contributed to the history and government sections of this book. She has a degree in modern languages and has written several dictionaries and textbooks for Hong Kong schools, had a column in the educational section of the *South China Morning Post*, and is the author of *Escape, a Story of Wartime Hong Kong*, written for Hong Kong teenagers.

VICKIE CHAN is a Hong Kong-based writer, illustrator/artist, and creative director who was educated and grew up in the United Kingdom. After a lifetime of traveling between West and East, she settled in Hong Kong in 2006. Since then she has written for the *South China Morning Post*, *China Daily*, *Gafencu* magazine, and the Hong Kong Trade Development Council, among others. Her main focuses are on art and design, education, culture, lifestyle, travel, and digital.

The Culture Smart! series is continuing to expand. All Culture Smart! guides are available as e-books, and many as audio books. For latest titles visit

www.culturesmart.co.uk

The publishers would like to thank **CultureSmart!**Consulting for its help in researching and developing the concept for this series.

CultureSmart!Consulting creates tailor-made seminars and consultancy programs to meet a wide range of corporate, public-sector, and individual needs. Whether delivering courses on multicultural team building in the USA, preparing Chinese engineers for a posting in Europe, training call-center staff in India, or raising the awareness of police forces to the needs of diverse ethnic communities, it provides essential, practical, and powerful skills worldwide to an increasingly international workforce.

For details, visit www.culturesmartconsulting.com

CultureSmart!Consulting and **CultureSmart!** guides have both contributed to and featured regularly in the weekly travel program "Fast Track" on BBC World TV.

contents

contents

Map of Hong Kong

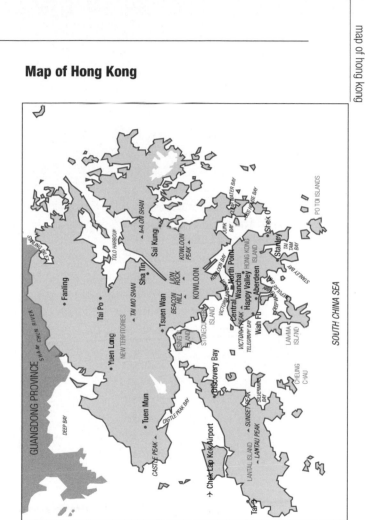

introduction

Hong Kong is unique. Its geography and history have given it a surprisingly important role in the world. Its historic role as a primary link for the world to China and the outpost of the West in the East is still relevant, despite the opening up of China to Western companies and competition with Singapore in certain industries.

Culturally, Hong Kong is rooted in the traditions of China, but there is more than a patina of Westernization. Nearly all the population have come to the territory in the last hundred years, most from southern China, but substantial numbers from the rest of China, from the rest of Asia, and from beyond. They came to a well-run, orderly place and found its comparative stability and the rule of law conducive to the oldest profession—trade.

Trade is everywhere. In addition to the myriad shops and stores, street markets and food stalls operate around the clock. Trade is the lifeblood of Hong Kong, and talk is the oxygen that fuels it.

The Hong Kong people are many and various. The substantial majority are Cantonese, entrepreneurial and industrious people from the farms and villages of the huge neighboring province of Guangdong. They brought with them a varied cuisine that is often acknowledged as "the best in China," seeing themselves as the French do in Europe. Their style is

open and extroverted compared to the more dignified
and serious northerners. Restaurants and shopping
malls overflow with families and groups of friends,
talking incessantly and missing no opportunity for
a bargain. In the unlikely event that a Hongkonger
is alone for a few brief moments, he or she will be
engaged with their cell phone. Silence is not a
preferred option.

Taking their style from the Cantonese, other settlers
from around the world have come to trade and prosper.
There are more holidays in the Hong Kong calendar
than in any other place in the world, and most holidays
are celebrated in the streets or in the parks, out with
friends, snacking and having fun.

This guide will give you a quick "in" to the
multifaceted community and way of life of this vibrant
territory. You will find helpful advice on business
and meetings, and on social etiquette. You will find
the confidence to participate rather than merely to
observe. In even a short trip, you can become part of
the community life of the Hong Kong people. Private
life, however, is a different matter. It is something few
outsiders ever share, and it is a real privilege if you do
become an insider. In this guide, we hope to give you a
few pointers to gaining closer access to it.

Key Facts

Official Name	Hong Kong Special Administrative Region of the People's Republic of China, or Hong Kong SAR	Cantonese name: *Heung Gong*. Mandarin name: *Xiang Gang*
Main Districts	There are 18 districts, the most well-known being Central & Western and Wan Chai on Hong Kong Island; Yau Tsim Mong, Kowloon City; Sham Shui Po, Kowloon; and Tsuen Wan in the New Territories.	
Area	411.68 sq. miles (1,066.53 sq. km)	
Terrain	Mountainous to hilly, with over 200 rocky islands and a natural harbor	
Climate	Tropical monsoon. Cool and dry in winter, warm and rainy in spring, hot and humid through summer, warm and sunny in fall	
Population	Just under 7.4 million	Probably the highest density in the world at 6,800 people per sq. km
Ethnic Makeup	92% Cantonese-speaking Chinese, 8% other	
Average Age	43.6	
Life Expectancy	84 years	
Adult Literacy	92%	
Languages	Written: Traditional Chinese and English (official). Spoken: Cantonese (official), Mandarin, some English (official)	
Religion	No official religion: Taoist, Buddhist, 10% Christian, 1% Muslim	
Government	Special administrative region of China with limited democracy	The head of government is known as the Chief Executive.

Constitution	Hong Kong has its own mini-constitution, called the Basic Law.	The legal system is based on English common law.
Per Capita	GDP US $36,000	
Currency	The Hong Kong dollar HK $1 (pegged at roughly 7.8 to US $1) is divided into 100 cents.	Notes: HK $1,000, $500, $100, $50, $20, $10. Coins: HK $10, $5, $2, $1, 50c, 20c, and 10c.
Media	The government company RTHK produces news and public information programs in Cantonese, Mandarin, and English. There are 9 radio channels, and 3 commercial free-to-air TV networks, namely TVB, RTHK and HKTVE. There are 10 TV channels. Cable TV available, incl. BBC, Bloomberg, and CNN. Netflix is available.	
Media: Press	The most influential Chinese-language newspapers are *Ming Pao*, the *Apple Daily*, and the *Oriental Daily*. The main English-language newspapers are the *South China Morning Post* and *The Standard*.	
Electricity	220 volts, 50 Hz	Same voltage and three-pin plug as the UK. Transformer needed for 100-v appliances
Internet Domain	.hk	Only available to registered companies and managed by the government
Telephone	The country code for Hong Kong is 852.	Emergency services: 999
Time	Hong Kong is 8 hours ahead of GMT.	

chapter one

LAND & PEOPLE

TERRAIN

The territory of Hong Kong consists of a peninsula and over two hundred islands, most of which are scarcely more than lone rocks. It is situated near the mouth of the Pearl River, which flows through the province of Guangdong from Guangzhou city (formerly Canton). Central to the territory is Hong Kong Island, facing the Kowloon Peninsula across the harbor. The airport, along with a great deal of new development, is on Lantau, the largest of the islands. Always short of land for building, the Hong Kong government has reclaimed enormous amounts of the shoreline over the years, and the harbor is considerably narrower now than it was fifty years ago.

The whole of the territory is a mere 411.68 square miles (1,066.53 sq. km)—including the sea—but into this small area is packed a population of nearly 7.4 million. The urban districts include some of the densest areas of population on earth, piled into towering skyscrapers that in turn are packed together like books along a shelf. This doesn't look as unattractive as it sounds. In fact, Hong Kong is considered one of the most beautiful of modern cities. The central urban area has a dramatic setting around its deep and busy harbor, and the steep mountains behind it form a grand backdrop to the soaring city blocks.

The main city, formally called Victoria but referred to locally as Hong Kong Island or Hongkongside, is the oldest colonial settlement. From the nineteenth century it had its cathedral, its governor's residence, government offices, and bank headquarters. It now occupies a strip along the whole north shore of Hong Kong harbor, merging with former villages and dormitory suburbs. Behind Central (the modern business district) rises the Peak, the highest point of Hong Kong Island, into whose steep sides have been inserted perilously narrow skyscrapers. These have some of the most extensive

views possible in any city, across the harbor to the hills separating Hong Kong from the neighboring province of Guangdong.

Opposite Hong Kong Island, Kowloon extends for miles along the shoreline. Previously the poor relation of the Island, it is the center of most of the commerce and has large residential areas. Formerly, small manufacturing enterprises in dingy factory zones were widespread, but in the last twenty years the majority of these have moved to mainland China. Imaginatively designed parks, shopping malls, and leisure complexes have been built in their place.

The Ninth Dragon

Where does the name Kowloon come from? Hills are characterized as animals such as dragons or phoenixes. The dragon also signifies the emperor. The name Kowloon is an anglicization of *gau lung*, which means "nine dragons." There were only eight hills guarding the Kowloon peninsula to the north, and a legendary emperor was so upset when he discovered this that he threw himself into the sea. He, being an emperor, had been the ninth, but he had not realized it.

On the Kowloon Peninsula are six other large cities, usually referred to as "new towns," since they were built only in the late 1970s. They are in the area known as the New Territories (see pages 25 and 30, below). The new towns, are often impressive new developments compared with the previous market towns but maintain a local feel compared with denser city areas in the territory. These are now largely residential, with commercial malls and some industry.

It comes as a surprise to many visitors that Hong Kong combines one of the busiest and buzziest cities on earth with expanses of mountain and sea where you can walk for hours and not meet a soul. There are sandy beaches and secluded woodlands. Stunning views extend around every corner. Outlying islands are comparatively quiet, and can be quite rural. Forty percent of the land mass is designated as country parks or nature reserves. These areas are planned to be exempt from new building, although a few encroachments have occurred.

The natural vegetation of the territory is subtropical, with a low scrub of bushes and small trees covering the gentler slopes. Fine old trees still exist in small pockets, but the occasional typhoons have inflicted a great deal of damage to the tallest. In recent years a number have been felled by the government—amid a small public outcry—in order to avoid the pressures of conservation and safety. Flowering plants and cultivated shrubs do very well, and the parks are full of color.

CLIMATE

The climate is classified as tropical monsoon. From January to April the weather is cool, but it heats up quickly after that bringing a lot of heavy rain. The summer is hot and humid. The humidity can be quite trying for people from cooler regions, and there is the added annoyance of mosquitoes in some areas. Most buildings and public transportation are air-conditioned, sometimes ferociously, which is a boon in such a crowded place. But by the fall the weather is starting to cool down and dry out, and the best months are October, November, and December, when it is usually clear with sunny days and cool nights.

AVERAGE TEMPERATURE (Fahrenheit/Celsius)		
	High	**Low**
January	64°/18°	57°/14°
February	63°/17°	55°/13°
March	72°/22°	63°/17°
April	77°/25°	70°/21°
May	82°/28°	75°/24°
June	86°/30°	79°/26°
July	90°/32°	81°/27°
August	88°/31°	81°/27°
September	86°/30°	79°/26°
October	82°/28°	75°/24°
November	75°/24 °	68°/20°
December	68°/20°	59°/15°

Typhoons

The word "typhoon" comes from the Cantonese *daai fung*, which means "big wind." These are typically tropical storms or cyclones and, according to the scale managed by the Hong Kong Observatory, only officially become a hurricane when wind speeds are at the most extreme. Hong Kong often has typhoon warnings, but direct hits are comparatively rare, occurring about once in two years. The warnings are important, and the strength of the typhoon is graded—numbers 1 to 3 (T1–T3) are not very significant, but next on the list is number 8 (T8), and when this is posted everyone leaves work or school and goes home to avoid extremely high winds, which are strong enough to move parked cars and blow pedestrians over. After that, the number 9 (9) denotes an increasing gale and 10 (10) denotes a hurricane and is raised very rarely. The sea becomes very rough (ferries are cancelled if a T8 or Black Rain signal is posted). The actual warnings are shown in the lobbies of public buildings, but most people get their information from TV and radio, or a notification via an app on their smart device.

THE PEOPLE OF HONG KONG
The Cantonese

Almost all the population of Hong Kong are Cantonese (*gwong dong yan*), named after the province of Guangdong. The Cantonese are one of the dozen or so main ethnic and linguistic groups in China. They belong to the dominant major group (constituting the large star of the five on the national flag), the Han Chinese. You may sometimes see them called *boon dei* or *punti* (people), which literally means "locals."

The Cantonese, like many southerners in the northern hemisphere, were generally smaller and darker than more northerly Han Chinese, who occupy the center and northeast of the country.

The Cantonese have a reputation among their compatriots for shrewdness and business sense. With the huge success of Hong Kong in the last fifty years, this reputation has grown in the world at large. Along with the Shanghainese, they dominate business in China.

Northern Chinese also tend to regard the Cantonese as unintellectual, loud, and overexcited in public, much as northern Europeans have traditionally viewed Mediterranean peoples. Certainly if you walk into a Hong Kong restaurant you will find the decibel level extreme, and looking around at the animated faces, in parties of friends and families, all talking at the tops of their voices, you might wonder who ever thought that the Chinese were inscrutable.

The Cantonese are also famed within China for their food, and their willingness to eat anything "that turns its back to heaven." Because of the history of Hong Kong, the Cantonese constitute the largest percentage of Chinese that you will find in other countries, particularly the British Commonwealth and America.

The Hakka
The Hakka are not now a very distinguishable minority of the population of Hong Kong, but their origins are not Cantonese and they were until recently a distinctly poorer, rural group, sometimes even characterized as gypsies. They had migrated from central to southern China in various waves to escape, for example, the Mongolian and Manchurian invasions and other earlier ethnic pressures.

The term "Hakka" was not originally a designation for a different ethnic group living in a particular area, but indicative of their status as "guests" who had left their homelands, in contrast to residents originally from the area. They later acquired the nickname "Jews of Asia," reflecting these mass migrations and the Hakkas' pioneering spirit. They also have a certain heroic quality in Chinese history: they are said to have escorted the Song royal household as it fled the Mongolians to Guangdong and fought bravely and died courageously in battles with the Mongolian armies. There are many Hakka among the overseas Chinese in the region and an estimated three million in Taiwan.

The Rest
About 8 percent of the population are expatriates, not including other Chinese groups such as northerners, Shanghainese, and in particular Chiu Chow, a group from just up the coast (and therefore sometimes defined as Cantonese) who are known as hard workers and drinkers of strong oolong tea.

Expatriates from all over the world are found in many professional and business areas, and number about half a million. In one international secondary school it was estimated that the children came from over eighty different ethnic groups.

An important minority is that from the Indian subcontinent. This group is better integrated than the Westerners—many of the younger members speak fluent Cantonese—but at the same time it suffers racial discrimination from the Chinese, in part because of color. The Indians rival the Cantonese in business ability, importing from the subcontinent and trading in the region. Most of the successful Indian businesspeople are Hindus from the province of Sindh, now in Pakistan. After independence, the Hindu community moved mainly to Mumbai (Bombay) and thence to the rest of the world. You can often recognize a Sindhi because many of their surnames end in "—ani." The Sindhis are big in import–export, mainly clothing and textiles. Their extensive families spread around the world and tend to intermarry, making ever-larger business networks.

There are also Sikhs, many of whom are descended from those brought in as police by the British, who knew the fear that a bearded, heavy-set giant of a man with a fearsome expression could inspire in the comparatively small and beardless Cantonese. There are Pakistanis, whose ancestors were also traders or police. During the past ten or twenty years professionals from the Indian subcontinent have come into Hong Kong as educators and specialists.

Filipino, Malaysian, and Thai workers also have a distinctive presence in the territory. The women are popular "domestic helpers" with Chinese and expatriate families alike. In recent years, an increasing number of Nepalese have been employed in restaurants and bars.

LANGUAGES

The official languages of Hong Kong are Chinese—spoken Cantonese and written traditional Chinese—and English. Spoken Mandarin or *Putonghua* (*pou tung waa* in Cantonese), meaning "common language," is also widely accepted. The written language in Hong Kong uses traditional Chinese characters, while in the mainland a simplified form has become standard.

The written language is not phonetic. Each character represents a word and has a specific meaning, although not all characters are strictly pictograms. You will often see people sketching characters on their hands with their fingers when trying to explain a word to a person from another dialect group. Having a common script is extremely useful in a huge country like China, and serves to unify the people more than any other cultural feature. Hongkongers generally understand simplified Chinese, but someone from mainland China cannot understand traditional Chinese script without learning it. Taiwan also uses traditional Chinese; Singapore and Malaysia use a simplified script, which differs slightly.

The spoken word varies far more than the written. Mandarin, based on the Beijing dialect, is the official spoken language of China. Cantonese is a colloquial variant spoken in Hong Kong and over the border in Guangdong Province. An example of the difference is that "Beijing" is the Mandarin pronunciation, and "buk ging" the Cantonese—which is why the British called it Peking. Cantonese also has a formal version, typically used in primary education, newspapers, and literature, which is closer to the Mandarin syntax, but not generally used in conversation (or films and television). Many phrases cannot be written at all. It's these aspects that make Cantonese more difficult to learn than Mandarin, on top of the wide use of slang and guttural tones.

Cantonese

There is evidence that the spoken Chinese of the Tang Dynasty (618–906 CE) was closer to Cantonese than Mandarin, the reason being the historical recurrence of China being attacked from the north, thus pushing the defeated leaders south as far as Guangdong. Classical Chinese poetry is pronounced closest to its meaning in Cantonese. However, this should not be taken to imply that the Cantonese are generally literature lovers or intellectuals: in fact the Cantonese, and especially those in Hong Kong, have a reputation for being "peasants" with a more materialistic than intellectual approach to life compared to the people of the north and east.

About 98 percent of the population speak Cantonese—*gwong dong wah*—as their mother tongue. It is also the language of most of the popular films from the 1970s onward, notably *kung fu* movies, and has its own pop music, called Cantopop. Cantonese is a tonal language. The intonation or "song" you use when speaking varies according to the word and not according to your mood or the emphasis you want in that sentence. Cantonese has more tones than any other Chinese language, which makes it especially hard for a foreigner to learn. (See also page 156.)

Other Chinese Dialects

As well as these two forms, other Chinese dialects can be heard, notably that from Shanghai, where many immigrants came from in the 1950s. In Shanghainese there are some sounds that are not found in any other Chinese dialect, so you may notice that it sounds different from Cantonese. It also has its own words and phrases. Taiwanese and Hokkienese from Fujian Province are also heard. Like Cantonese, they tend to have more richness and color than an official language such as Mandarin.

English is the preferred language of business between non-Chinese, or between Chinese and other groups. English is usually the prevailing language if there is a dispute over a bilingual contract. The sizeable Indian population are mostly from Sindh, and speak Sindhi at home, but their English is fluent and they are usually educated at English-speaking schools. Many Japanese and Korean businesspeople live in Hong Kong, and there is a Japanese international school. Likewise, French and German speakers have their own international schools.

A Bilingual Society?
You might think that Hong Kong would be the ideal bilingual society. Street signs and government forms are presented in English and Chinese, and both languages are highly visible. Yet it has been shown that if two languages are used so extensively, there will be two monolingual cultures. There is no call for Chinese to read English, or vice versa. Visitors often compare the English of Hongkongers unfavorably with the rest of China. For a language to succeed, it has to be useful, and for most Hongkongers, English is only marginally useful. Likewise, few expatriates learn more than their address and basic useful phrases in Cantonese.

A BRIEF HISTORY

There can be neither safety nor honour for either government until Her Majesty's flag flies on these coasts in a secure position.
(Captain Charles Elliot, 1839)

Hong Kong did not feature in early Chinese history in any special way. A few villages, fishing as well as

agricultural, grew up. The typical Cantonese shape—
walled and square—can still be seen at Kam Tin in the
New Territories. Hong Kong's excellent harbor, deep and
well protected, was only discovered in the nineteenth
century by the British. The name of the whole territory,
heung gong in Cantonese, means Fragrant Harbor. It was
named for the fragrant camphor wood that was exported.

After the Opium Wars, the Chinese ceded Hong Kong
Island to the British. They colonized it as part of the
Chuen Pi Treaty (1841), revised by the Treaty of Nanking
(August 1842), ending the first Opium War.

The Opium Wars
The two mid-nineteenth century Opium Wars
between Britain and China (Britain joined by France
in the second one) were as much about equality and
opening up trade with China as about opium. The
Manchu Chinese emperors banned their people from
importing any goods. Because the Europeans were
eager for Chinese exports—porcelain and tea being
the most important—an imbalance of trade resulted.
Opium, a narcotic, was already smoked in China, but
Britain increased the market for it by importing large
quantities produced in their colony of India. It was the
most profitable product traded in the British Empire at
that time. The Chinese government tried to stamp out
both import and consumption, and in 1837 sent a senior
official to Canton, the main importing center. Stores
of opium were burned, and this became a *casus belli*,
justified on Britain's side by its free trade philosophy. Two
wars ensued—in 1839–42 and 1858–60.

The Chinese overestimated their power against the
modern war machinery of the West, and were forced into
humiliating treaties (now called the Unequal Treaties)
establishing privileged rights for foreign traders in newly

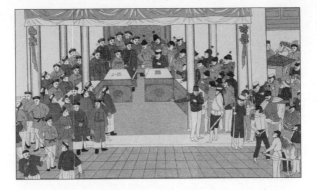

designated "treaty ports." These treaties were naturally highly resented in China, and because of them Hong Kong's right to a separate existence was always denied by the Chinese government. Of course, most treaties are unequal in the sense the Chinese meant, one side being stronger than the other. In hindsight, even Chinese historians acknowledge that the treaties benefited many ordinary Chinese people by opening up their country to the modern world. But this did not diminish the importance of Chinese resentment at the existence of Hong Kong and other treaty ports.

"A Barren Island"

Hong Kong was not an obvious prize of the first Opium War. In fact, Britain's Foreign Secretary, Palmerston, dubbed it "a barren island with hardly a house upon it," and sacked Charles Elliot, the first governor, and author of the quotation introducing this section, for the weakness of the treaty and the apparent uselessness of Hong Kong.

At that time, Portuguese Macau was the only European town in China, and it traded with China via Canton (Guangzhou), the only city on the south coast, then and now. The Portuguese had been developing Macau as a port since the fifteenth century; but the harbor is shallow, and the Portuguese government did not have the means to make much of its links to its other colonies, such as Goa and Melaka. Hong Kong very quickly replaced it in importance. By 1860, twenty years after the founding of Hong Kong, the head of the British Colonial Office declared it "Another illustration of 'the art of colonization,' . . . and the success is such as to show the flexibility of the present system—or want of system." This was the year in which Kowloon, "long considered a sort of neutral ground" (Governor Davis) and Stonecutters Island, adjacent to it, were added to Hong Kong by the Convention of Peking after the Second Opium War.

The area beyond Kowloon, including all the other islands, was not added until 1898. The British wanted this land, which they called the New Territories, to protect the port of Hong Kong and the entrance to the Pearl River from pirates by sea and raids by land. Significantly, it was granted to them (by the Peking Convention) only on a ninety-nine-year lease, which had enormous repercussions in 1997.

The British Empire and Colonies
The British Empire had its origins in the sixteenth and seventeenth centuries. Britain was at that time using its naval traditions to bolster trade and emigration, particularly to North America. India, being the richest and largest colony, was run by the East India Company, but there was a gradual expansion in the eighteenth and nineteenth centuries of ports and land directly controlled by the British government. Other European countries, especially France, fought Britain for possession of, for example, the West Indian sugar-producing islands, but Britain was the major colonial power in the nineteenth

and early twentieth centuries when the empire was at its zenith. Its colonies were ruled by governors appointed in London. Initially many had military backgrounds, but gradually a cadre of civilian "colonial officers" was developed. These officers entered through highly competitive exams, being posted between colonies for three to five years at a time. Interestingly, this meritocratic system of preferment by exam was taken from the old Chinese administrative system, which the British greatly admired.

India, itself termed an Empire, was governed separately by the Indian Civil Service, which native Indians joined increasingly into the twentieth century, becoming the majority by independence in 1947. From then on, it was only a matter of time until the British Empire was broken up and the countries within it became self-governing. Hong Kong was the only colony not to gain full independence.

The Administrative Service
Hong Kong followed the colonial model, with specialist training in written Chinese and spoken Cantonese given to its recruits, known as "cadets." The cadets had the benefit of at least one posting in another colony, as well as four or five promotions through the ranks in Hong Kong. Local Chinese joined the Administrative Service, as it was called, later than elsewhere, but by 1997 constituted the majority of the total of four hundred.

Half the expatriate Administrative Officers left in 1997, but the service remains the fundamental elite of government. With entry by a tough competitive exam, interview, and group tests, three thousand graduates apply every year for thirty places. Thus the colonial system of government continues uniquely under China's Communist regime.

By 1898, Hong Kong had become one of the leading ports in Asia and one of the most successful colonies in the empire. There was a considerable exodus from Hong Kong and Guangdong at this time to Australia, the United States, and the Straits Settlements (today's Malaysia). The recruitment and dispatch of migrants was one of its major activities in the nineteenth century.

Hong Kong had diversified while continuing to grow as an entrepôt to China. But still it lagged behind Shanghai, which was better placed, in the middle of the eastern coast. Shanghai was less strictly controlled by the Colonial Office, with an "International Settlement" government led by expatriate businessmen. Hong Kong was the quieter center, right through to the absorption of Shanghai into China in 1949. Its growth socially as well as economically was steady, however. Missionary societies such as the London Missionary Society and the Morrison Education Society developed education that was vital for providing the junior members of the government as well as filling the gaps in middle management in the substantial local businesses that had developed, such as Jardine Matheson and John Swire.

Colonial Governors

Hong Kong was governed during its one hundred and fifty years of British rule by colonial governors. Many had had experience in other colonies, such as Malaya, the West Indies, or Ceylon. Some were notable eccentrics.

Sir John Pope-Hennessy (1877–82) was a colorful Irish governor, renowned for liberal views and a quick temper. He was an intelligent man, and notably pro-Chinese, making himself very unpopular with the expatriate community for promoting Chinese in the political system.

Sir Murray Maclehose (1971–82) was governor during the period of Hong Kong's greatest expansion and development. He inherited a colony whose reputation for corruption, especially in the police force, was legendary, and in 1974 founded the Independent Commission Against Corruption (ICAC), which had wide-ranging powers, including the ability to investigate any government servant who appeared to be living above

his means. Its effectiveness led to Hong Kong becoming one of the least corrupt societies in the world, and serving as a model to other governments wishing to improve their own reputation in this regard. He was a committed environmentalist, and a 62-mile (100-km) walking path in the New Territories is named the Maclehose Trail after him. Maclehose initiated the talks on the future of Hong Kong with the mainland government, paving the way for the handover to China.

Chris Patten (1992–7) was an enthusiastic democrat, which resulted in clashes with the mainland government during the vital five years before the handover; but his democratic style endeared him to local people, and he was often seen with his family in public places.

However, there was a noticeable gap generally in society between the Chinese and the expatriates: "It is extraordinary—not to say discreditable—that after fifty-five years of British rule, the vast majority of Chinese in Hong Kong should remain so little anglicized." (Governor Hercules Robinson, 1895). Some of this non-anglicization was deliberate, and related to legislation demanded by the expatriates for segregation via different house-type—European housing and Chinese housing. The main example of this segregation was the Peak, the mountain in the center of Hong Kong Island, which was reserved for, and is still dominated by, European housing.

Some segregation was caused not by racism but by understandable medical concerns about the spread of disease. Malaria and other fevers were widespread, and even today many of the world's major epidemics start in southern China, where people and animals live in close proximity.

In general Hong Kong was well and fairly, if not democratically, governed. There were problems that defeated the government, one being the Triad societies, organized criminal gangs with pseudo-religious rules that still exist today.

Triads

Triads are the world's biggest organized crime group. Their origin lies in the resistance to the Mongol invasion and conquest of China in the thirteenth century. They were an underground force that overstayed its welcome when the Han Chinese retook power under the Ming dynasty. They developed their own language for coded communication and religious ceremony. As in organized crime elsewhere, they were involved in controlling illegal gambling and prostitution. There were an estimated fifteen thousand Triads in the late nineteenth century when an attempt to make membership of a Triad society punishable by branding was vetoed by the British home government. In the 1950s they became involved in illegal immigration, and controlled various trades such as the interior decoration of the new housing estates. They operated through intimidation, most dangerously linked through some members in the police. By the end of the twentieth century the police had managed to wipe out Triads from their ranks, and the takeover by the mainland, where the near elimination of Triads had been one success of early Communist rule, lessened the evil generally.

The Dilemma of Democracy

The question of democratization was another classic dilemma, too much even for governors with democratic or pro-Chinese instincts such as Pope-Hennessy.

Nevertheless, the movements in China for a less autocratic government highlighted Hong Kong's relative liberalism compared to the mainland. In 1899, "It was assumed that the knowledge of the just treatment of the Chinese inhabitants of Hong Kong and British Kowloon would induce the population of the leased area [the New Territories] to accept the jurisdiction of Great Britain with equanimity if not with pleasure." This was Governor Henry Blake on the takeover of the New Territories. In fact, there was some physical resistance by the local leadership, especially the Tang clan of Tai Po and Yuen Long villages, because they were proudly Chinese and quite contented with their agricultural lifestyle rather than the unequal society of the British colony. The New Territories were lightly governed, and were used as a buffer zone against immigration as much as militarily, and were not developed until the 1970s.

Nearer to the heart of Hong Kong, there was long-term argument about Kowloon Walled City, a village in the north of the Kowloon Peninsula that had been used as the local Chinese officials' ("Mandarins") base next to Hong Kong and about which the 1898 treaty regarding the New Territories was vague. It was not actually governed by the British until the 1980s, and it meanwhile became a notorious refuge for criminals.

KOWLOON WALLED CITY

Originally a military fort, the Walled City became a Chinese enclave in the New Territories after they were leased to Britain. It was largely demolished by the Japanese during the Second World War. After the war, and with an influx of immigrants from China, squatters took over and it became a haven for criminals and drug addicts. The Triads ruled the roost until the mid-1970s, when a police crackdown diminished their numbers and power.

By the 1980s, the City had a population of about 50,000, and a crime rate far below the Hong Kong average, despite the lack of any law enforcement. It was home to hundreds of medical practitioners who had none of the qualifications necessary to work in Hong Kong itself—notably bonesetters and tooth pullers. Many local Chinese consulted these physicians.

In 1993, the whole tottering edifice was destroyed, but not before a Jackie Chan movie, *Crime Story,* was made using the deserted interior, with its maze of dark passages. The area has now been turned into Kowloon Walled City Park. Designed to resemble a Qing Dynasty garden, its centerpiece is a *yamen,* or hall, which houses a photographic exhibition.

The Early Twentieth Century

The pressure for Britain to take the New Territories came from the international strategic concerns at Russian and French expansion in Asia. The international tension continued until the defeat of the Russians by the Japanese in 1905 and the new alliance of the British with the French, the Entente Cordiale, of the same year.

By this time Chinese events were making a significant impact on Hong Kong. The desire not to come into conflict with the Chinese government led to the expulsion, in 1896, of one of the leaders of revolt against the Manchu rule—Sun Yat-sen, who had been educated as a doctor in Hong Kong. After his expulsion there was sympathy for his cause, and in the next such case to be discussed, that of the liberal reformer Kang Yu-wei, the decision went the other way: he was given refuge when his revolution failed after a hundred days in 1900. In 1911 the revolution led by Sun Yat-sen had initial success, but it took a long time, until 1928–9, to cover the whole of China, and from then on the Japanese were threatening from the east, starting with the seizure of Manchuria in 1931 and Shanghai in 1932.

Sun Yat-sen came back to Hong Kong as President of China to speak at the university congregation in 1923. He spoke out in appreciation of Hong Kong and British colonialism: "Afterwards [after his medical training in Hong Kong] I saw the outside world, and I began to wonder how it was that foreigners, that Englishmen could

do such things as they had done, for example with the barren rock of Hong Kong."

Hong Kong was struggling a bit in the interwar period, with the decline of Britain and its doctrine of free trade. In 1931 Britain was forced off the gold standard by economic circumstances, and on to a system of imperial preferences, a protectionist policy based on imperial connections. This did not suit Hong Kong, which was more a free trader in and out of China than a producer of anything.

Japanese Occupation

During the 1930s, the dominance of Japan assumed paramount importance in both China and Hong Kong. This became a real threat once the war with Germany began in 1939, because Japan was allied to Germany under the Axis Pact (1936). However, there were still many British in Hong Kong who underestimated the Japanese, because of their physical stature, lack of sporting ability, and nationalistic immaturity. It came as a complete surprise, therefore, when, in the early hours of December 8, 1941, and simultaneously with

Pearl Harbor, Hong Kong was attacked. The Japanese quickly overran the New Territories—the newly built Gin Drinkers fortified line had to be abandoned for lack of troops. Next came Kai Tak airstrip and the catastrophic sinking of the two battleships, *Prince of Wales* and *Repulse*, on their way from Singapore to help.

Kowloon fell in five days but the governor, Sir Mark Young, rejected surrender. The Japanese then landed on the middle of the island on December 18, advancing

quickly over it to Repulse Bay, and forced a surrender on Christmas Day after a Japanese ultimatum wishing the British troops a happy Christmas!

The treatment of military prisoners and expatriate civilians, who were put in the same camps, was bad, as Japanese culture did not honor surrender. Many died of starvation or ill treatment. The Japanese also oppressed the local population, and the majority were forced by lack of food to move back across the border, bringing the population down from 1,600,000 to 600,000.

It was a ragged territory, the object of American bombing against the Japanese, that emerged from this occupation on August 30, 1945, with the arrival of the British Pacific Fleet.

Postwar Developments
It was lucky for British Hong Kong that it was not the American fleet that got there first. The Americans were a real threat to Hong Kong as a British colony: President Roosevelt believed that the self-determination clause in the Atlantic Charter (the forerunner to the UN Charter) applied to British colonies as much as to German, Italian, and Japanese ones. He pressed for Hong Kong to be

given to Chiang Kai Shek's (Jiang Jieshi) China. However, Churchill, strong on the British Empire, hung on to it.

Nevertheless it was a new world that Hong Kong faced after the war, and the Labour government that replaced Churchill's wartime coalition was not enthusiastic about the Empire, wishing to bring Hong Kong up-to-date in terms of democratic government. The governor, Sir Mark Young (1941–7), who had been imprisoned in Japan during the war, was strongly in favor of some measure of democratization. A measure, called the Young Plan, was approved by London. This ensured the legislature would be half elected by the Chinese population and half by the foreign population.

This was not enough for some, but the reason it was not followed up in the next governorship, that of Sir Alexander Grantham (1947–57), was ironically the changes in China—the civil war between Chiang Kai Shek's Nationalist Government and the Communists under Mao Tse-tung (Mao Zedong). The violent takeover by Communism in 1949 and the survival of a highly armed Nationalist Taiwan worried the leaders of the local community in Hong Kong, who feared that elections would be taken over by these two extremes. They asked that the Young Plan be postponed.

Events in China affected Hong Kong in a more direct way—there was an enormous influx of refugees, which doubled the population in five years. A major fire on Christmas Day, 1953, in one of the squatter areas that had grown up around the city, caused a big policy change. The biggest public housing program in the world was launched. It housed as much as half the population within the next thirty years.

The new population provided cheap labor for the transformation of Hong Kong from an entrepôt port into a manufacturing center, providing cheap goods such as toys, wigs, and textiles to undercut rivals such as Britain and other rich countries. Indeed the rapid development of Hong Kong put it on a level with Britain in GDP per head by the late 1980s.

Thirty people a day were "legally" entering Hong Kong during this time, and as many as a hundred illegally. Hong Kong may have been the only place in the world where the legitimate incoming population was chosen not by its own government but by the "exporting" country, China. Continuing immigration necessitated a great deal of social provision in the latter half of the twentieth century, when standards of health, housing, and education were usually compared to Britain's rather than to China's.

Politically there was still no change in favor of democracy because of fear of the continuing extremism and instability across the border overflowing into Hong Kong. Mao Zedong in fact left Hong Kong alone, even when the anarchy of the Cultural Revolution spread to the colony in 1967. There were riots, and some policemen and rioters were killed. It was said that Mao and in particular his pragmatic deputy, Chou En-lai (Zhou Enlai), saw the continuance of Hong Kong as a useful outlet for Chinese goods and an equally useful entrance for imports.

The Handover

While China had recovered from the Cultural Revolution by the end of the 1970s under the newly pragmatic leadership of Deng Xiaoping, it was the British side that felt it had to change things in a major way. In 1983 Prime Minister Margaret Thatcher began formal negotiations with Deng on the future of Hong Kong because of the approaching expiry of the ninety-nine-year lease on the New Territories. Thatcher wanted to negotiate for the return of only the New Territories, as stated by the agreement, but was told that they could not be separated. Reservoirs and new towns had been built there, and Hong Kong Island and Kowloon were not viable without them. So she caved in and the whole territory of Hong Kong was promised back to China by the Joint Declaration of 1984. In Beijing to sign the document, Thatcher tripped on the steps of the Great Hall of the People, symbolizing to the Chinese either British disarray or merely "bad joss" (the fates against them). The Joint Declaration promised that Hong Kong would retain its system and autonomy, under Deng's slogan, "one country, two systems."

It had been thought too dangerous to institute self-government before the future was clarified—China was less threatened by a colony than by a democracy. Even though all other colonies had been given independence from Britain by the 1980s, Hong Kong therefore had to make do with a partial (district-level) democracy at first. Even when the Legislative Council was democratized, it did not have the crucial power of choosing the Governor's Executive Council, which remained appointed by the Governor through the transfer to China in 1997 and beyond under the Chief Executive.

Although democratic elements in Hong Kong, such as the Democratic Party led by Martin Lee, and independents like Christine Loh, were not happy with the semi-democracy provided at China's insistence, they acknowledged that it ensured a stable and prosperous transfer of power from Britain to China in 1997 and in the early years of Chinese rule.

This transfer of power went smoothly, a lot more so than had been expected eight years before. In 1989, events in China affected Hong Kong as never before or since. A major student-led movement in China arguing for democracy and against corruption was crushed by military means in Tiananmen Square, Beijing. Hong Kong people, to the tune of an estimated two million, came out into the streets in protest. Fears of what would happen in Hong Kong when it was absorbed into China led to increased emigration, particularly of liberal middle-class residents. Half the remaining expatriates in the Administrative Service, for example, who were fully entitled to stay, left before 1997 largely for reasons of concern over the post-1997 political prospects.

On June 30, 1997, the handover of Hong Kong to the People's Republic of China officially took place. A short ceremony was held at the Hong Kong Convention Centre. Prince Charles, representing the Queen, and the Chinese President Jiang Zemin made speeches, and the British and colonial Hong Kong flags were lowered. Just after midnight on July 1,  the Chinese flag and the Hong Kong Special Administrative Region flag (a bauhinia flower in white on a red background) were raised. Hong Kong is now officially known as Hong Kong Special Administrative Region of the People's Republic of China, or Hong Kong SAR.

SINCE THE HANDOVER

As it turned out, China was very careful in the first years of sovereignty not to break the Joint Declaration or interfere with the status quo. This was a tribute to the mainland's pragmatism inherited from Deng; to the balancing role played by the first Chief Executive (the old position of Governor); and to the firmly defensive position of Anson Chan, the Chief Secretary (head of the civil service and deputy to the Chief Executive) appointed by the last Governor, Chris Patten.

Ironically, until recently Hong Kong has had fewer problems where they were most expected—in the political arena—and most in economics, which had been predicted to go smoothly. The downturn was a regional rather than a specific problem, but it has been exacerbated by the marginalizing of Hong Kong as a business center now that China, with much cheaper labor and a somewhat casual attitude toward health, safety, and environmental regulations, has become a major player in the commercial and financial world.

Tung Chee-hwa, the first Chief Executive of Hong Kong Special Autonomous Region, came to Hong Kong from war-torn Shanghai with his family when he was ten years old. He went to a British university and spent time in America, and had been in business for the thirty years before his appointment. He was apolitical, and somewhat scholarly, making him a generally acceptable choice of leader, tending to foster the image of "Uncle Tung." Critics complain that he did nothing positive in his tenure but it is difficult to see what he could have done with the Beijing government towering in the background—a situation that continues to be apparent within Hong Kong politics.

Despite a previous fear of China, Hong Kong people have shown themselves to be relatively robust politically, some continuing to elect democrats to the Legislature, while others back the establishment (pro-Beijing) camp.

A proposed law to penalize "crimes against the state" made hundreds of thousands of Hong Kong people come out in protest in July 2003, blocking streets for six and a half hours. According to one protester, the law was so wide-ranging that anything could be punished. The march against the anti-subversion legislation eclipsed ceremonies marking the 1997 handover to China. Chief Executive Tung gave assurances that his government would continue to take active steps to maintain and safeguard rights and freedoms. By September the bill had been withdrawn in order that it be rewritten in a way that was more acceptable.

The Joint Declaration signed by the British and the Chinese had stated that there would be a direct election for the successor to Tung. In 2005 when Tung resigned, Donald Tsang became Chief Executive, having already been given approval by China and stood unopposed by the 800 appointed members of the Election Committee.

The 2014 Umbrella Revolution
In 2007, the second Chief Executive, Donald Tsang, said that he would resolve the question of universal suffrage. The National People's Congress Standing Committee ruled that the ultimate aim was for the Chief Executive's election in 2017 to be decided by universal suffrage. In 2014, however, it was announced that the candidates for Chief Executive would be nominated by a nominating committee, allowing two to three candidates from whom the people could choose.

A class boycott by students across the city ensued, formally under two movements known respectively as the Hong Kong Federation of Students and Scholarism. They were also joined by a third movement called Occupy Central with Love and Peace (Occupy Central), led by Benny Tai Yiu-ting, Associate Professor of Law at the University of Hong Kong. The boycott culminated in a seventy-nine-day protest, which coalesced around three main sites. The primary site was located in Admiralty, outside the Central Government Building and Tamar, blocking an important highway, which forms part of the main corridor across Hong Kong

Island's business district. Smaller protests also formed in Causeway Bay and Mong Kok, the most crowded area in the region. The latter saw aggressive clashes between pro-democratic (or "localist") supporters, pro-Beijing citizens, and frustrated Mong Kok business owners and minibus drivers.

The situation was compared to the 1966 riots, which centered around an increase in the Star Ferry fare. Scenes of the police using tear gas on largely peaceful crowds stunned many in Hong Kong, a city where the focus is usually on business and making money. Despite the international attention the Umbrella Revolution gained, China's General Secretary, Xi Jinping, limited his public statements about the situation while remaining inflexible. A committee of members of parliament from the UK were advised that they would be turned away if they tried to enter Hong Kong to look into the situation—which the chairman of the British Parliament's Commons Foreign Affairs Committee described as "overtly confrontational." Chief Executive, Leung Chun-ying (known as CY Leung) was told to end the situation as quickly and peacefully as possible.

While the situation on the streets was eventually resolved, the question of Hong Kong's right to genuine universal suffrage remains unanswered. A number of talks were held between the government and key student figures from the 2014 protests, but primarily as a sop the protesters. The 2016 Legislative Council elections saw a total of eight (of 35) seats taken by "localists," but the majority is still held by pro-Beijing councillors, and the position of Chief Executive remains pre-approved and is voted for by 1,000 key figures.

GOVERNMENT AND POLITICS

The present government of the Hong Kong Special Administrative Region is in the hands of the Hong Kong business establishment and is fully endorsed by the Chinese government. It is not an elected government: it has been appointed by China in several stages at different times, but, that aside, it is not very different from the system brought in by the British.

The business of government is done by career administrators (Administrative Officers, or AOs) who are responsible for thinking up, initiating, and putting policies into practice. Executive Officers (EOs) are responsible for enacting the policies and managing them. They are supported by clerical and technical staff. It is a lean government, with comparatively few bureaucrats as a proportion of the population.

The government is led by the Chief Executive (formerly the Governor), who presides over the Chief Secretary (head of the Administrative Service), the Secretary for Justice (head of the Judiciary), and the Financial Secretary.

AOs have a lot more power than they would in a democracy, but this is shaped and checked by the

politicians who make up the Legislative Council. The makeup of Legco (pronounced "Ledge-co") has varied over the years, but despite efforts in the 1990s, notably by Chris Patten, to democratize it further, it remains a body that is only partially directly elected. As in the mainland, elections are restricted. Candidates are chosen largely by the administration; Chief Executive contenders are pre-selected and approved by China, and only 1,000 key business people and those of importance are allowed to vote. Legco consists of 70 members, with 35 members returned by geographical constituencies through direct elections, and 35 members by "functional constituencies" voted for by designated legal entities such as organizations and corporations and "natural persons" (approved individuals). These functional constituencies were created by dividing the population (but not all of it) into areas of expertise or influence, such as education, labor, or law. On a local level, each of the eighteen districts of Hong Kong has a District Office (Administrative Offices and Executive Offices) and a District Board (elected).

In practice, there is comparatively little politics in Hong Kong, although this has increased in the last decade. The media and some Legco members are critical of the administration, and filibustering has become a feature of Legco, which is primarily split between those wanting democratic rule and the pro-Beijing camp. Compared to the space and effort devoted to political matters in fully democratic countries, however, there is very little debate. Whether this comes from apathy or the tendency of Hongkongers to keep a prudent silence on matters controversial and their focus on making money and prospering, is hard to say. A book of cartoons published in 1997 by American cartoonist Larry Feign had the title *Let's All Shut Up and Make Money*, and it remains typical of the Hong Kong attitude.

HONG KONG'S PLACE IN THE REGION

Hong Kong was important in the last half of the twentieth century for being the gateway to China. Goods and people streamed through the port and airport in both directions, leaving a thin film of money in Hong Kong on every trip. This role has, of course, largely declined since the rest of China has opened up to trade and tourism. However, Hong Kong remains an important international business center in the region.

While China continues to open up to both foreign business and tourism, Hong Kong remains a comfortable and safe destination in the region, as its rule of law, seeming social equality, and welfare stand out against successful but more corrupt and harsh regimes around it. It offers traditional Chinese culture in a highly palatable dose, while also providing the ability to retreat to an impressive range of Western cuisines, modern comforts, and fairly little need to speak anything other than English. It also remains a safe and free place to trade and do business, within a transparent legal system and tax-free conditions.

Hong Kong is one of the semi-democratic, successful Southeast Asian nations that were known in the 1990s as the "four little dragons"—Hong Kong, Singapore, South Korea, and Taiwan—next to the big dragons, China and Japan. Countries like Malaysia and Thailand look to Hong Kong (though they might not admit it) as a model of a place that has achieved social harmony with prosperity. Hong Kong's one big rival in the region is Singapore—independent and democratic, but with a reputation for an unnecessarily tough government and a sanitized style of life. Singapore has traditionally seen Hong Kong as corrupt (which it was, until the 1980s), too obsessed with money, and dissolute. The Cantonese film industry has done little to modify these beliefs. By contrast, Hongkongers think of the Singaporeans as lazy, not properly Chinese, and boring.

In recent years, however, Singapore has done well in attracting and maintaining overseas businesses, and with the opening up of China making it more directly accessible, Hong Kong could be overshadowed in the future. While Hong Kong still focuses on its original outstanding industries like finance, shipping, and manufacturing (via China), Singapore has done more to diversify, supporting the development of newer, rapidly changing industries such as technology and digital, creative servicing, and even television.

VALUES & ATTITUDES

THE CHINESE WAY

The Hong Kong Chinese are proud of being Chinese, and most of their customs are very similar to those of the mainland. But a hundred and fifty years of British rule did influence them, and the trade-linked prosperity of the last thirty years has Westernized them.

To outsiders, at a glance, Hong Kong seems to epitomize middle-class life. For the most part, people are soberly behaved, industrious, and believe in the "bourgeois" values of education, hard work, and providing for the family. It is difficult to tease out the

strands of traditional Chinese from those of traditional Western attitudes, since they have much in common.

Much social behavior both within the family and outside has come down from Confucius, the Chinese sage of the sixth century BCE. Confucius was an idealist, who taught the importance of social order and justice. It was very important to him that rulers should behave as rulers should, their people as peoples should, fathers as fathers, sons as sons. This has led to the strong element in Chinese behavior of obedience and conservatism. Filial piety is a peculiarly Chinese term, and refers not only to the pious deference of a son to a father but also of the employee to the boss, the person below to the person above, in all dealings. When the Hong Kong delegation negotiating the handover agreement went to Beijing, they were openly told that their correct attitude would be that of a son craving indulgence from a father.

Traditionally, the elderly are accorded great respect and elderly parents often live with one of their children rather than in a retirement home. Elderly women are fondly referred to as *po po* and elderly men as *yeh yeh*, meaning granny and grandpa. Likewise, those who are older than you and close to your parents' age can respectfully be referred to as aunty—often said in English—and uncle, which can also be said in Cantonese: *ah sok*. Most Chinese provide for their parents in their old age as a matter of course, and can receive a small tax deduction for doing so.

In the bustle of Hong Kong, some of the respect toward the elderly is less evident, but passengers usually give up seats on public transportation to the elderly, and bus drivers will often patiently tell elderly passengers to take their time as they get on and off. Passers-by often help an elderly person negotiate a difficult sidewalk or step. But it's just as common to see elderly people working hard in local markets or sorting through trash, collecting tin and paper to sell for recycling, in order to make ends meet. There is a lack of provision for the elderly who cannot rely on their families, which is perhaps one of Hong Kong's more obvious oversights in social welfare.

With a focus on filial piety, behavior toward bosses is also different from that of most cultures. There is much more quiet acceptance, especially in front of others, and a general desire not to offend, even at the price of truth. For example, a definite statement made on a political point will be agreed with, whatever the private feelings. If you are a client, you can expect much the same attitude toward you, which can sometimes result in problems not being raised, or being told "yes" when in fact the answer is "no."

The more aggressive and egalitarian behavior of Westerners is tolerated and has had some influence in Hong Kong, but it is still better for foreigners to be aware of the primacy of social harmony in their dealings with the Hong Kong Chinese. Arguments are taboo, although mainland Chinese tourists are known for their sometimes loud and aggressive behavior toward service staff. If you come across such an incident, you will notice Hongkongers nearby stunned into silence, and listening. Similarly, Honkongers are known to be reticent, even in academic circles where vigorous debate is the norm in most societies. One consequence is that asking questions is rare—for many, it is better to continue in confusion than to clarify or question—and thinking outside the box remains rare. In a survey of the importance of certain virtues in the workplace, nearly all Hong Kong office workers ranked harmony well above hard work, efficiency, attention to detail, and honesty.

Foreigners will find that formal invitations are taken seriously by the Chinese in Hong Kong. Such entertaining is often done outside the home—mainly due to the modest size of many people's homes— ususally in a restaurant or members' club, which requires careful planning. If you are invited to someone's home, particularly for a family gathering, regard it as an honor. If the Chinese are invited for dinner they will tend to bring, for example, a bottle of whiskey, not wine, and may expect a feast in return. Generally, the invitation would come from a superior to an inferior, which enforces a feeling of obligation. An extravagant present will remove the social obligation to return the invitation directly.

Certain attitudes are regarded by the Chinese as foreign, and therefore undesirable. There is little tolerance of overtly extravagant or unusual lifestyles or behavior, although in practice the Chinese will not be overt in their disapproval, so it may go unnoticed by the foreigner. Certain public conduct that is generally tolerated in Western culture is disapproved of by Hongkongers. In general, the Chinese don't suffer displays of emotion. This includes kissing and displays of intimacy, especially between those of the same sex, losing one's temper, drunken behavior—in fact, anything extreme—although younger generations are becoming more Westernized in this respect. Being openly gay is still taboo for most Chinese, who might be more accepting of a Western friend who is gay. In general, the Chinese are outwardly tolerant for the most part and silent about that which they disapprove of. They view themselves as moral and hardworking, and are proud of their traditions.

By contrast, much social behavior that foreigners would consider rude might be tolerated, or is even the norm among the Chinese. This includes speaking to strangers in an abrupt, "no-frills" way (which may, to a foreigner, seem rude) as well as mocking and criticizing a foreigner's attempts to speak Chinese—neither of which are meant as racism; laughter at apparently inappropriate moments, which covers embarrassment and indecision about what to do; carrying on loud conversations on cell phones; hawking and spitting in the street (a decreasing occurrence); and having general disregard for the environment. All these aspects of everyday Chinese behavior are sources of irritation for many visitors.

LUCK AND SUPERSTITION

As we shall see in the sections on *feng shui* and astrology in Chapter 3, the courtship of Lady Luck and the thwarting of evil spirits play a conderable role in everyday life. Young people have not generally rebelled against the traditions associated with this—wearing new clothes at Chinese New Year, sweeping ancestors' graves at Ching Ming and burning offerings, consulting the Chinese Farmer's Almanac for the best days to carry out both business and personal activities, and doing what is deemed necessary to bring luck in business ventures. Superstition is still a strong part of Chinese culture in Hong Kong and any actions that are believed to generate luck and generally please and respect the ancestors, spirits, and gods are considered important.

FACE

Understanding the concept of "face" is essential to succeeding in Hong Kong, both in business and in everyday social interactions. A person's reputation and standing rest on the concept of their "saving face." Their actions reflect not only on their company, but also on their family, and any other groups of which they are a member.

"Losing face"—causing yourself or someone else embarrassment or loss of self-possession, even unintentionally—can be disastrous, particularly for business negotiations. To be respectful you can "give face" by way of compliments and general agreement, combined with being personally modest and humble. Should someone you respect lose face in your presence, you can help them save face by counteracting—through words or actions—the thing that caused the loss. For example, by taking the blame for something that is not really your fault.

If, on the other hand, you feel that you have caused someone to lose face, it would be best to remain quiet and humble, even allowing others to "pay face" to that person, rather than to try to fix the situation yourself. In business, it is likely that the hierarchy in the room will be clear, but the nuances of face and detecting whether it is lost can be complicated, and can take time to truly understand.

Remember that you will lose face if you become angry, irritable, or upset in your dealings with Hongkongers. Aim to stay calm, measured, and non-confrontational.

THE BRITISH LEGACY

Many of Hong Kong's institutions are British in origin or in inspiration. The civil service in particular, having been designed and run by the British for a hundred and fifty years, continues to operate in a British style. The same applies to big business, especially in the top "hongs" or large business firms, led by "taipans," or big businessmen. Well-known hongs include Swire (which owns Cathay Pacific), Jardine Matheson, and HSBC. They are essentially Western with small elements of Chinese tradition, such as paying a thirteenth month of wages as a bonus at Chinese New Year or employing a *feng shui* expert to advise on a building.

In general, though, the British legacy is more modest than one would have thought, largely through the pride of the Chinese in their own traditions and the tendency of the colonial government to leave well alone.

Education is the area of greatest influence, since most of the early schools were started by missionaries and Churches. Later the government provided free schooling for all, although as late as the 1970s it lasted only until the age of thirteen. Unlike many of today's Western children, Chinese children bring to education a positive attitude, knowing that good marks and hard work is what their parents expect, thus ensuring a comfortable and successful future. The consequence is that the Western values put out by the school system and the government are often taken on board in a very Chinese manner. The antismoking campaign is a case in point. Schools and government advertising told the public not to smoke, for their own good. People gave up smoking in enormous numbers, so compared to the mainland Hong Kong is fairly smoke-free.

More abstract values, such as honesty and justice, although undoubtedly present from Chinese culture, have been given a Western expression and prominence. A sense of "the rule of law" has been picked up, mostly from the British, simply from the good experience gained from its being in force for a hundred and fifty years. It is high on the list of things that set Hong Kong apart from the mainland, and is guarded jealously by those who have seen how important it is in a fair society. This links with a disapproval of corruption that has made Hong Kong, with the help of the Independent Commission Against Corruption (see page 28), probably the least corrupt country in Asia.

Attitudes toward social justice have slipped into Hong Kong mainly by way of the missionaries and the education they provided. The Christianity promulgated by early British and Americans in Hong Kong had a strong social ethic, and schools and charities were set up by them and later by their admirers. Nineteenth-century institutions such as the Po Leung Kuk, a charity for rescuing young servant girls, were set up by Hong Kong Chinese along the lines of Western charitable establishments—even their buildings having a grave Victorian air. Trade unions and discussions of equality and rights are also Western imports, but they are still less developed than in most Western countries. Environmental issues, again a Western initiative, are largely ignored by the general public, but various organizations, and Legislative Councillor Christine Loh, are attempting to change this. Occasional government infomercials about recycling now grace Hong Kong television channels.

Inevitably, Hong Kong has a greater internationalism than the mainland. From its founding as a city, it was a trading post between the hugely differing cultures of Britain and China, and its attitudes are outward- rather than inward-looking. Businesspeople routinely travel around Asia and to the rest of the world, thinking no more of visiting Japan or Thailand for a couple of days than Americans might think of visiting a neighboring state. The universal concerns and discourse of international business are the common currency of their lives. In general, Hongkongers love to go overseas for vacations, and they are becoming sophisticated travelers. However, they are famous for preferring Chinese food whenever they can, wherever they are!

Since Chinese traditions and old-fashioned Western ones overlap in so many areas, it is safe to say that if visitors behave in a sober and restrained manner, this will be fine with the Hongkongers. And if they fail to be offended by the unintended rudeness of the Chinese way, they will enjoy life in Hong Kong more.

MEN AND WOMEN

The Hong Kong population has an imbalanced ratio of men to women, with only about 855 men to every 1,000 women. In the workplace, women are fairly well represented, with a notable drop in the female workforce around the ages of thirty to thirty-five. Their roles, however, are less equal. The number of men in management and medicine outstrips women by about 60 to 80 percent in most industries, with a large majority of women performing lower-paid clerical support work. The civil service in general, as well as politics, sees a more balanced ratio; however, Hong Kong is known to have one of the lowest ratios of women on boards. There is no obvious discrimination on the basis of gender, although women who work a full day outside the home are generally expected to cook, clean, and care for their children inside it as well (albeit sometimes with the aid of a domestic helper).

Men, on the other hand, can work late, entertain outside the home, and even travel for work, regardless of family responsibilities at home.

Domestic Helpers

Many middle-class women are liberated from the chores at home and enabled to do paid work by the existence of a huge number of immigrant "domestic helpers," mainly from the Philippines but also from south Asia and Thailand. Chinese families often wish to employ Filipinas, with their comparatively good knowledge of English, to look after their children and teach them the rudiments of the language. These workers were the first people in Hong Kong to have a minimum wage. They send most of their money back to their families, and they have fixed-term contracts, renewable every two years. They arrive on special visas and are required to "live in" with their employers, though this is not always the case, especially as families with smaller apartments increasingly prefer to pay for their accommodation elsewhere. Their traditional day off is Sunday—they are legally required to leave the home in order to ensure they are not forced to work—when they tend to dress up and congregate in the public spaces and shopping malls in cheerful, voluble groups, singing, eating, and chatting. Some Filipino men are employed as drivers and increasingly Filipinos are finding commercial work as gardeners, musicians, or wait staff.

Sexual Lifestyles

The Chinese have been reluctant to acknowledge homosexuality. Male homosexual acts were decriminalized in Hong Kong in 1991—while lesbian acts have gone unmentioned by the law—and in 2006 the age of consent was brought down to sixteen, in line with heterosexual sex. Publically, homosexuality still carries a stigma, which might be felt more by local Chinese homosexuals. Nonetheless, gay visitors are recommended to exercise cultural sensitivity and prudence in public places. Hong Kong has a significant gay community, with a number of gay nightclubs. It's vibrant, fun, and international nature has made it a popular destination for gay tourists in recent years.

ATTITUDES TOWARD WORK AND MONEY

Think of nineteenth-century industrialists in Britain and America, and you have something of the Hong Kong Chinese mentality when it comes to work and money. Work is not something to enjoy, but something that must be done. It is interesting that even for the industrious Chinese, once the money incentive has been taken away, work falls off. During the most stringent Communist rule in China, workers had no incentives to work harder. The Hong Kong Chinese dismissed them as lazy, and did not want them flooding in. Similarly, government service in Hong Kong was known as the "iron rice bowl" because it was so secure. Although most government workers were conscientious, some only put in the hours without working flat out. It is in business that the real work is done, because the rewards are directly linked.

Work is a commodity, and should take up most of your life and energy. It may be significant that the Cantonese for "go to work" actually means "go *back* to work," which implies that work is the normal and expected place to be. If you call an office early in the morning and the person you want is not there, you will be told, "He hasn't come back yet."

If you work hard enough, you will earn money, and money is the most important thing. Health and family are very important, but they are to some extent dependent on external factors, whereas money, in an economy like Hong Kong's, lies within the grasp of the individual.

Money is hugely important in itself; it is not particularly valued as a bringer of freedom or choice. More, it is the way of showing the status and importance of the family to whom it is accruing. Money is so well loved in Hong Kong that the most common Chinese New Year sayings center around making more money or business going well. Therefore it is the duty of everyone in the family to make as much money as they can. It can be spent on education—when it is seen as an investment for the future and can itself be a status symbol—or on things that clearly define status, such as precious objects, cars, fine clothes, and jewelry. In traditional Chinese society, a second or third wife or concubine was a public indication of wealth.

It is strongly believed that money should work for the family—it should be ploughed into investments and businesses. If it is in abundance, it can be given to charity, which will also increase the family's status, since the source of the donation will be publicly known. A hospital ward or a school hall, for example, will probably, and preferably, bear the name of its donor. Such an act also brings good fortune, just like the giving of red pockets or *lai see* at Chinese New Year (and birthdays).

The only anomalous use of money, to Western perception, is for gambling. True, the possible prizes may be very large, but the odds are usually so poor that it would seem a foolish enterprise to look on it as an investment. However, enormous amounts are spent on gambling each year by rich and poor alike, so the myth of luck prevails. Gambling has been such a passion for the Chinese that in Hong Kong betting is only legal within the Jockey Club betting branches. As a result, Hongkongers have always enjoyed a trip to Macau to visit the casinos there.

CLASS AND STATUS

Hong Kong has one of the largest divides between rich and poor, and while some residential areas are way beyond the means of those on lower wages there are large parts of the city where rich and poor live in close proximity, due to the nature of property development and urban renewal. Hongkongers are a peaceful people who prefer to mind their own business and there is no friction between the different classes. In this busy and compact city it is necessary to rub shoulders with one another, even if just on the street. Hongkongers prefer to focus on working hard and earning money; living in a relatively crime-free society removes any sense of fear, prejudice, or dislike for one another.

A sense of Chinese superiority is apparent in racial attitudes. While not common, you might occasionally see a Filipino or Indian worker being treated rudely. That many such workers can speak Cantonese further reduces the likelihood of such incidents.

ATTITUDES TOWARD FOREIGNERS

By and large, Hongkongers do not overtly show their dislike of others, and are more likely to ignore someone they don't want to interact with than to make a fuss. After years of British rule it should be no surprise that foreigners, particularly Westerners, are generally accepted, often with eager curiosity.

Attitudes toward foreign-born Chinese are more complicated. Those from Western countries at times complain of being judged for their "otherness" while others seem to fit right in. Meanwhile, mainland Chinese tourists tend to be louder and more pushy than Hongkongers and often stand out, and a shop assistant's disdain for them might be more visible, which is indicative of the sharp socio-cultural differences between Hongkongers and mainland Chinese.

In general, there is a sense of hierarchy within the many Asian races and skin tones, but this rarely has an impact on daily life. As mentioned above, domestic workers may sometimes experience racial prejudice.

chapter three

CUSTOMS & TRADITIONS

RELIGION

Chinese Temples

As in most modern capitalist cities, religion is not a large part of most people's lives. The temples are nominally Buddhist, but various other gods and goddesses are enshrined in them. There is also a strong Taoist element. Before Buddhism spread throughout China in the sixth century CE, each region had its favorite local gods and goddesses. Since there is no notion of a right and a wrong way to pray to the higher powers, these local deities can be found along with Buddha and various other Chinese gods in many of the temples.

In Hong Kong, the goddess Tin Hau is a special favorite. She is the goddess of the sea, with a protective

responsibility toward all mariners, and fishermen in particular. She is reputed to have been a fisherman's daughter who was kidnapped and taken in a ship far down the coast. A typhoon blew up, but she calmed the waters and saved the crew. There are many Tin Hau temples, particularly in the older fishing areas like Shek O and on the outlying islands.

Another favorite is Kwan Yin, the goddess of mercy. She is entreated by anyone with a problem, and on days when the state lottery is drawn many supplicants can be seen in her temples. There is a large statue of Kwan Yin and Tin Hau situated on the beach in Repulse Bay, which attracts a large number of locals and tourists alike.

On the island of Cheung Chau, one of the oldest fishing communities, Pei Ti, god of water and the Spirit of the North, is most revered. He is also supplicated by fishermen, since he has the power to still storms and give good catches.

Unlike the rest of China, Hong Kong has not had any breaks in the religious observances of its people. After the Second World War, many Chinese from religious institutions in China settled in Hong Kong, and several are still there. Buddhist and Christian monasteries

were established in the New Territories, particularly on Lantau Island. There is a large Buddhist community in the mountains there, and in 1995 the biggest Buddha in the world was erected on Lantau. It is a very popular place of pilgrimage—this is not a solemn occasion, but an excuse for an enjoyable day out in dramatic scenery. The monastery has a big temple and several gift shops, and offers a reasonably priced vegetarian lunch. Not that the average Hongkonger would eat only vegetables from choice. The special religious vegetarian meal is endured because it might confer merit, and even that includes chunky mushrooms and flavored bean curd that seem to imitate meat. Nominal Buddhists the Hongkongers may be, but vegetarian they are emphatically not—except for the most devout practicing Buddhists, who are vegan— as many visiting veggies have found to their dismay.

Chinese temples are very worldly. Families wander around them, and apart from taking their shoes off before entering the inner temple no particular observances are necessary. Silence is not strictly observed. Animals come and go unhindered. Apart from the smoke from the joss sticks, there is no odor of sanctity, solemnity, or mysticism. Most worshipers will light a

bunch of joss sticks and plant them into a sand-filled tub in front of their deity of choice, praying quietly as they do so. There is also a fortune-telling facility in larger temples. A cylindrical box full of long slivers of bamboo is used to obtain your fortune. On each sliver is a number. The petitioner shakes the box repeatedly, and after about half a minute, a sliver of bamboo inexplicably works its way up and out of the box. When it falls out, the petitioner picks it up and takes it to the priest for interpretation. The priest refers to a venerable book, in which each number has a prediction.

Religion, Philosophy, or Superstition?
Even if organized religion is not a great part of people's lives, the general philosophy of life evolved in China, with Buddhist, Taoist, and Confucian elements, underpins traditional life to some extent. A holistic approach to the body and nature underlies most people's beliefs. In traditional medicine, exercise, and eating, the concept of *chi*, or energy flow (see page 73), prevails.

It is also a truism that Hongkongers don't have a religion, they just have luck. Certainly there are a lot of quasi-religious practices that may be termed superstitions, particularly surrounding business and money. As you walk through the Hong Kong streets, you will often see huge flower- and ribbon-decked decorations arranged in front of a doorway. On closer inspection, you will see that a business is opening in that building today, and that the red or pink ribbons are inscribed with lucky wishes for the new restaurant or shop.

The business owner will have gone through many propitious deeds before the moment of opening. The *feng shui* (see below) of the building and of the space within it will have to be approved by a consultant. Furniture and ornaments will be chosen and placed with their recommendations in mind. Astrological predictions for the prosperity of the enterprise will be noted. Certain Chinese years (see Chinese Astrology, page 71) are more conducive than others to making a lot of money, and there is a relationship between your own year of birth and the current one to take into account. Numbers (see Numerology, page 69) are of importance too—an unlucky telephone number or car registration can be blamed for all sorts of business problems. Probably a traditional business owner will make a donation at the local temple, or even visit the big Buddha, just to tip the scales in his favor.

Other Religions
There are several flourishing Christian Churches and foundations in Hong Kong. Because of previous intolerance of Christianity in mainland China, several missions and religious bodies relocated to Hong Kong after 1950, and many are still there today. In addition, Christian schools and hospitals were established, providing good education and medicine at relatively low prices for the local population, and many of these schools are still regarded as the best in the territory.

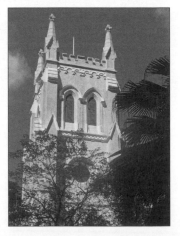

About 10 percent of the population belong to one of the Christian Churches. Anglicans and Episcopalians are served by the cathedral in Central Hong Kong, Christ Church in Kowloon, and several other churches. Catholics, whose numbers have been greatly swelled by the population of Filipina domestic workers, have their cathedral close to the Anglican one, and nearly fifty churches throughout the territory.

Baptists are so well represented that they have a whole university to themselves in Kowloon, as well as churches, schools, and a hospital. The Seventh-Day Adventists, too, have a college and two hospitals in addition to their churches. Latter Day Saints (Mormons) also have a strong following.

Islam is also represented in the territory, with six mosques. The Muslim community in Hong Kong numbers over 300,000. More than half are Chinese and many others are from Pakistan, Indonesia, and Malaysia.

Since the handover, religious freedom has continued to flourish, and the introduction of a holiday to mark Buddha's birthday has been seen as an improvement in relations between the government and religious bodies. Missionaries of all faiths can operate with no interference, and all the religious charitable institutions are thriving too.

FENG SHUI

In Cantonese, *feng shui* literally translates as "wind, water." Its general tenet, that man should live in harmony with nature, has spread its influence in the West in the last few decades. In its most basic application, *feng shui* is used to determine where to build a house, workplace, or temple. The compass was invented in China not for navigation, but for *feng shui*.

Hong Kong is the best place to find out about this four-thousand-year-old philosophy. The mainland Chinese government outlawed the practice of *feng shui* after the Revolution, in their bid to prevent "opiates of the people" sapping the drive to work hard for a Communist state. There is still official disapproval of anything regarded as superstitious. But in Hong Kong it flourished, and continues to do so. There are said to be more than ten thousand *feng shui* experts in Hong Kong and many of them have amassed tidy fortunes and glittering reputations—and even fame and status, for those appearing regularly on television or servicing local celebrities.

Through the ages *feng shui* has acquired many extra areas of influence, so that every aspect of living and working space is susceptible to its energy. A house with its back to a wooded hill (for shelter) with an open outlook to the south over water (for light and air) is regarded by most people—not just the Chinese—as more desirable than a house in a damp hollow with hills in front of it, exposed to cold winds at the back. A river or a pond will increase wealth—undoubtedly true for arable farms and for fish or duck rearing. Villages in the New Territories still have *feng shui* woods behind them, which will protect them from wind or landslides. Thus far the Western property developer would agree, but *feng shui* goes much further than this. It addresses not only a building's proximity to natural features and other buildings, but also the shape and material of the building, shapes of rooms, positioning of doors, windows, and furniture, and even where in a room flowers or trinkets should be put. And it is all to harness the power of luck.

In Hong Kong, *feng shui* is widely practiced, and *feng shui* masters are in great demand and extremely well paid. At first glance, you might see that an astonishing number of buildings may benefit from the basic requirements of "hill behind, water in front," as the steep slopes of the Peak on Hong Kong Island and the hills of Kowloon and the New Territories provide just that. However, it can also be seen that buildings are crowded into the flatter areas with a concentration that no other city can match. Of necessity, these buildings are not sited in auspicious places, so the original tenets of *feng shui* have been stretched and bent to accommodate the needs of the people to maximize their luck.

The World's Most Expensive Tree?

Not only hills and rivers provide *feng shui* protection. Trees are important too. When Swire Properties were planning a huge shopping complex at Pacific Place, over the Admiralty MTR station, they encountered problems with a 130-year-old banyan tree, solidly rooted in the middle of their proposed development. They promised that it would be preserved at all costs. Cost was right—the "concrete flower pot" that eventually had to be constructed around it cost around HK $24 million (about US $3 million)—not counting the time spent by staff on its upkeep!

Although Central, the modern business district, is regarded by *feng shui* experts as adequately protected, the original area of British commerce was not so lucky. It was in a flat and mosquito-infested marshy area, misnamed Happy Valley. There was a bad outbreak of malaria in the mid-nineteenth century, which the Chinese workers living there blamed on the inauspicious *feng shui*. Gradually, business moved to the luckier area a couple of miles down the road.

The area of Central where most banks and prestigious firms have their headquarters is reputedly situated on a dragon's vein, which brings a lot of luck and wealth. When the Hongkong and Shanghai Bank was built, great care was taken to make the most of this lucky vein. The shape of the bank apparently suggests a laughing Buddha, and the governors of the bank ensured a clear view to the harbor (and the money it represents) by paying for a recreational square and underground parking in front of it. Escalators taking visitors to the main banking hall are strangely curved— again for *feng shui* reasons.

Uphill from the Hongkong Bank, and also on the rich vein, is the Bank of China, designed by I. M. Pei. The design is, however, not respected by *feng shui* experts. It is based on triangles, which are inauspicious in themselves. It is to the surroundings that the bank presents the most menace, however. In particular, it has a very sharp corner pointing directly toward Government House and the former Central Government Offices. Such a corner is thought to be like a dagger pointing at the heart of the Hong Kong administration. Before the advent of the Bank of China, Government House was auspiciously located and oriented. Could it be that even in the early days of British rule, *feng shui* was taken into account?

Another corner of the Bank of China points toward the former Legislative Council building—now the Court of Final Appeal. As if that weren't bad enough, the two projecting masts, or "chopsticks," on top of the building point upward, resembling nothing so closely as the incense sticks used to honor the dead.

Color schemes, rearrangement of furniture, and other measures can counter chronic bad luck. Moving house or offices is a last resort in hard times.

Westerners in Hong Kong have also succumbed to the "insurance" mentality of *feng shui* believers. You may as well get it right, just in case. When Marks & Spencer first came to the territory, it didn't do very well, but after the *feng shui* expert had recommended tactically placed lights, wooden turtles, and fish tanks, sales picked up. A branch of McDonald's in Kowloon is reputed to have a tank of piranha fish—quite a draw in itself, one might think, as a curiosity!

The Hong Kong Tourist Association offers *feng shui* tours of some of the most obvious landmarks of this ubiquitous practice.

Mirrors and Water
Luckily, a relatively cheap means of protecting yourself against neighboring buildings and other inauspicious things exists. All you have to do is hang a small, hexagonal mirror, called a *bat gwa* mirror, in such a way that it reflects the bad luck back to its source. The theory is that an evil being will be repelled by seeing itself in such a mirror. Making sure the sea or other water is reflected in a *bat gwa* mirror, on the other hand, can increase the financial fortunes of a company. Since water represents money (and *soy*, water, is the slang term for money), you may notice that most banks and businesses have water features somewhere about the buildings, or at least a fish tank in the lobby.

NUMEROLOGY
Numbers have always fascinated scholars, and Chinese numerology is complicated and subtle. It goes with *feng shui*. Personal numerology is usually based on birth date, but numbers come into everyday life in many ways, and all the numbers in your life have significance.

The sort of numerology that visitors may come across in Hong Kong is centered in the sounds of the words in Cantonese:

Yi (two) sounds like the word for "easy."
Saam (three) sounds like the word for "alive," or "lifelong."
Sei (four) sounds like the word for "death."
Baat (eight) sounds like the word for "prosperity."
Sup saam (thirteen) sounds like "sure life."

By extension, twenty-four sounds like "easy to die," and so is considered very unlucky; 28 sounds like "easy prosperity," so is very fortunate; 138 sounds like "prosperity all your life," and 168 like "everlasting prosperity"—and you can't get luckier than that.

CHINESE ASTROLOGY

Like its Western counterpart, Chinese astrology divides people into twelve basic types, although there are several subdivisions. Instead of being based on the month and date of the year in which you are born, the Chinese system looks at the year of birth. Each year is named after an animal, and begins at Chinese New Year—between one and two months after January 1. Each animal has its own characteristics, which are not always the ones you might expect.

The Twelve Animals

As with Western astrology, the origins of the twelve-animal system are lost in the mists of time. There is a charming legend, however.

The Jade King of Heaven was feeling a little bored, and decided he wanted to see some representatives of the animal kingdom on Earth. Envoys announced that the first twelve to reach him would be most highly favored.

The first to be invited were the Cat and the Rat, who were the best of friends. The Cat decided to take a nap before the race to see the Jade King so he asked his friend the Rat to wake him in time. Instead, the Rat left the Cat to sleep—so they are now sworn enemies! Ten other animals were invited to join the race: the Ox, the Tiger, the Rabbit, the Dragon, the Snake, the Horse, the Goat (or Ram), the Monkey, the Cock (or Rooster), and the Dog. They duly appeared and presented themselves in front of the Jade King's palace; but the King noticed that there were only eleven. An envoy was sent down for another animal, and the first thing he saw was someone carrying a Pig, so that was added to the others.

The Rat, inclined to show off, hopped on to the back of the Ox, and played a tune on his flute. The Jade King, impressed, gave Rat the first place in the line, followed by the patient Ox. He liked the courage of the Tiger, and put it third, and then the rest in order: Rabbit, Dragon, Snake, Horse, Goat, Monkey, Cock, Dog, and Pig.

So every twelve years there is a new cycle, starting with the Rat, who is the cleverest in the zodiac. However, in Vietnam, they claim that the Cat took the year that the Chinese give to the Rabbit! But their characteristics are the same.

The characteristics of people born in different years are, roughly, as follows:

Rat: clever, charming, imaginative; can be conspiratorial.

Ox: straightforward, kind, patient; can be dull.

Tiger: courageous, loyal, honorable; can be critical.

Rabbit: diplomatic, peace-loving, intuitive; can be indecisive.

Dragon: magnetic, dynamic, lucky; can be intolerant.

Snake: elegant, self-contained, perceptive; can be obstinate.

Horse: enthusiastic, flexible, cheerful; can be impatient.

Goat: creative, sensitive, imaginative; can be irresponsible.

Monkey: independent, sociable, shrewd; can be manipulative.

Cock: flamboyant, obliging, resilient; can be vain.

Dog: humane, tolerant, idealistic; can be anxious.

Pig: easy-going, sympathetic, sensual; can be spendthrift.

Because the Lunar New Year starts on a different calendar date each year, it is difficult for people with January and February birthdays to calculate their animal year without a special table. For the others, it is enough to know that the Year of the Rat started in early 1900 and recurs every twelve years.

There are five elements in the Chinese system, and therefore each year has a secondary name: Earth, Fire, Water, Metal, and Wood. Each combination recurs only once in sixty years. The year 1966 was the year of the Fire Horse, and children born in this year are thought to be wild and uncontrollable. There were significantly fewer births in Hong Kong that year than in the other years in the decade.

Each year has its own character, and astrologers in Hong Kong are quick to point out the advantages and disadvantages of each year as it turns. For the record, there have been about 4,714 Chinese years to date.

TAI CHI AND *CHI GUNG*

You might, if you are an early riser or plagued by jet lag, find a surprising number of people out and about at 6:00 a.m. The parks and open areas will certainly be host to groups of people, many of them elderly, practicing the ancient art of *tai chi*. Originally, like most of the three hundred different styles of bodywork,

tai chi was a martial art. It emphasizes stability of the body, and does not have the high-energy kicks of the *kung fu* movies. *Tai chi* (translated as "great ultimate") is characterized by being gentle and yielding. You can become mesmerized watching the slow, focused movements. They have the qualities of a flowing river, yielding to the solid and fixed, sweeping away the weak and unstable.

Chi, or *qi*, is the energy flow within all living things, sometimes defined as "that which distinguishes the living from the dead." If this flow is blocked, weak, or out of balance, you will become ill—physically, mentally, or spiritually. The term *chi gung* or *qigong*, means "*chi* work" and is used as a blanket term for all exercises that work on the *chi*. It works from the outside of the body inward—so that when you have done the regime of physical exercises, you should be feeling healthier internally, both in body and spirit. It is "a path and not a destination," so is practiced as a daily ritual to ensure a healthy, balanced life. It may be said that the Chinese believe in *chi* as a kind of universal life force, and that this force has been externalized in other cultures and named "God."

The Origin of Tai Chi

Tai chi is alleged to have been founded by a Taoist mystic and hermit, Chang San-feng, who probably lived in the thirteenth century in central China. The legend has it that Master Chang was out walking in the forest when he saw a snake engaged in a fight with a crane. Chang was impressed at the ingenious way the snake was able to feint, elude, and counterattack the large, powerful bird. That night, the art of *tai chi* came to him in a dream.

FESTIVALS AND HOLIDAYS

Hong Kong people work hard, but their calendar is liberally sprinkled with holidays, both Chinese and Western. Employees are entitled to twelve statutory paid holidays a year (from the the list below) and there are several additional celebrations throughout the year.

January 1	New Year's Day
January/February	Three days at Lunar (Chinese) New Year
March/April	Ching Ming Friday and Monday at Easter
May 1	Labor Day
May	The Buddha's Birthday
May/June	Tuen Ng (Dragon Boat) Festival
July 1	Hong Kong SAR Establishment Day
September	Day following the Mid-Autumn Festival
October 1	China National Day
October	Chung Yeung
December	Chinese Winter Solstice, Christmas Day, and Boxing Day

Some of these holidays are discretionary, which means that a company is not legally required to give staff official leave. Any holiday that falls on a Saturday will take place on the Saturday. Any holiday that falls on a Sunday will usually take place on the Monday after, at the government's discretion. When two holidays coincide (for example, Good Friday or Easter Monday and Ching Ming), usually an additional working day will be given as a holiday, at the government's discretion.

Chinese New Year

By far the most important festival is the Lunar or Chinese New Year, which marks the beginning of spring. Beware of planning anything at this time—most people do not work over the three days, and banks and businesses, including some restaurants, will be firmly shut. Chinese New Year falls on a different date each year, but it corresponds to the new moon between mid-January and mid-February, and lasts three days.

As in Scotland, the first person you meet must bring you luck. In Hong Kong's case, a red-clad person would be especially lucky. Red or colored songbirds are also a good omen.

The first and second days of the celebrations are a time for family reunions, and the streets are quiet on these days. Traditionally, a religious thanksgiving for Heaven, Earth, and the family accompanies the gatherings. The most important focus of this is the union of the ancestors with the living members of the family. Ancestors are deeply respected, because they laid the foundations of each family, and are felt to be still with the family in spirit. They are honored with a special New Year's Eve dinner. On the third day of New Year, people can leave their families and go out and have fun.

The New Year symbolizes sweeping away the old and adopting the new. Debts must be paid and houses cleaned by the end of the old year, so that a new start can be made. Clean during the first days of New Year and you will sweep away all your luck and fortune. On the stroke of midnight on New Year's Eve, every door and window in the house must be open to allow the old year out. Firecrackers and other fireworks welcome the new one in.

There is a feeling that anything that happens on the first day of the year will continue for the whole year. So positive language and laughter are encouraged, and arguing, crying, and dwelling on the past are avoided. Children and younger relatives as well as unmarried friends are given *lai see*, little red pockets with crisp new banknotes inside, for good fortune. Patriarchs of families and important people in the community will have dozens of these red pockets at their disposal so that they can dispense good fortune far and wide.

Probably more food is consumed during the New Year celebrations than at any other time of the year. On New Year's Day, Chinese families eat a vegetarian dish called *jai*. Other foods include a whole fish, to represent togetherness and abundance, and a whole chicken for prosperity. Noodles should not be cut, as they represent long life. Sweet desserts made of glutinous rice are very popular in Cantonese cuisine and *tong yuen*, a round ball filled with sesame paste, is eaten at Chinese New Year to symbolize family togetherness.

Ching Ming and Chung Yeung

Also known as the Grave-sweeping Festival, or Spring Remembrance, Ching Ming takes place at the third moon. Chinese families visit the graves of their ancestors to clear away weeds, tidy the area, light incense, and make offerings of wine and fruit. The day is celebratory in feel—more like a picnic than a solemn memorial. It is the most widely celebrated day for ancestral remembrance.

Chung Yeung, which occurs six months later, is Fall Remembrance, so much the same sort of thing happens. It is also traditionally good to go up into the hills at Chung Yeung, because there is a legend about a man who was advised to take his family to a high place for the ninth day of the ninth month. When they returned, they found that their village had been destroyed by enemies.

Buddha's Birthday
Worshipers show their devotion by washing Buddha's statues. Vegetarian meals are eaten. Celebrations center on the major temples and monasteries in Hong Kong.

Cheung Chau Bun Festival
This is special to Hong Kong. It takes place at the full moon of the fourth month, usually in May. The villagers of Cheung Chau, an island with an ancient fishing community, erect huge bamboo towers near the Pak Tai Temple. On the towers are fixed sweet buns together with effigies of three gods. For three days the islanders become vegetarian. On the final day a colorful procession winds through the village streets. Children, elaborately costumed and made up, are supported on tiny seats held up by adults. They look as though they are standing on top of poles. They make their way to the temple where, for safety reasons, the old practice of climbing the towers to seize the buns has been discontinued. The buns are now distributed in a more orderly fashion after a religious ceremony.

Tuen Ng Festival
This has now become known internationally as the Dragon Boat Festival, although the races were inaugurated only in 1976. Over a hundred teams from across the globe participate in the waters around Hong Kong. After the locals have raced, the event becomes an international open. The main competitions take place on Shing Mun River in the New Territories and Stanley on Hong Kong Island, which is particularly popular with corporate teams. Teams of twenty-two or twenty-four paddle their long, elaborately carved, colorful boats to the beat of heavy drums. The boats have dragon's heads and tails.

The festival commemorates the death of a popular national hero, Qu Yuan, who drowned himself in the third century BC, in protest against a corrupt government. As locals tried to rescue him, they beat drums to scare fish away and threw dumplings into the sea to keep the fish from eating his body. During the festival, people eat rice-and-meat dumplings wrapped in bamboo leaves.

Mid-Autumn Festival

Another excuse for a family reunion occurs on the fifteenth day of the eighth month of the lunar calendar. This is the Mid-Autumn Festival, Moon Festival, or Lantern Festival. The full moon's shape symbolizes the family circle. The special food associated with this festival is a moon cake, a sweet, heavy cake with a filling of sugar, fat, sesame, lotus seeds, walnut, and a golden salted egg yolk, which is reminiscent of the moon. Modern forms include a custard version and a frozen version that comes in flavors from traditional, like egg custard and lotus, to modern, like chocolate, mango, and cheesecake. To eat their moon cakes, families gather on hillsides, carrying colorful paper lanterns in various animal or

vehicle shapes, and view the moon. The day after is the statutory holiday, because it is the tradition to stay up late in order to celebrate within the view of the moon.

Prohibitions

Hong Kong has plenty of warning signs everywhere, and there is no excuse for ignoring them. There are quite a number of different prohibitions, although the sign of a pig with a red line across it ("No animals") that used to decorate the MTR in the early days has, alas, gone. Metallic balloons are still banned from the MTR, and an announcement is often aired in stations as a reminder. It might seem strange, but a helium-filled Mickey Mouse once floated into a tunnel during rush hour, causing chaos.

Many public places and offices as well as the MTR ban smoking, so ask before you light up or you might be fined.

LITTLE POINTS OF ETIQUETTE

- Toothpicks are like networking—used at every meal. Put your left hand discreetly over your mouth—in the manner of someone shading eyes from glare—while the other hand cleans the teeth.
- Don't show the soles of your feet to others. Putting your feet on a chair, or on a train seat, is regarded as very bad manners.
- Traditional Chinese will train their left-handed children to use their right hand when eating with chopsticks. Sit at a crowded round table with everyone eating, and you'll see why!

- Don't leave chopsticks vertically in your bowl. It's a reminder of incense sticks in a bowl of ashes—a sure reminder of death—and an action used to threaten someone.
- Give and receive business cards, and other pieces of paper, with both hands. One hand looks casual to the point of rudeness.
- Some members' clubs do not allow flip-flops or thonged sandals. Others do not allow sneakers or even jeans and shirts that do not have collars. Be sure to check in advance if there is a dress code, although clubs are relaxing such policies.
- If you are invited to a wedding, it is appropriate to give money in a red pocket (envelope) or *lai see*, not objects. The idea is to cover the cost of your meal, although this is not a strict rule. If the recipient is a colleague or someone you manage, ask a reliable colleague to tell you the appropriate amount to give.
- It is considered polite to refuse an invitation or gift once, and then to demur and accept it gracefully.
- Displays of affection, temper, or anything "extreme" are frowned upon.
- White is the color of death, and black and white on a flowered display panel commemorate a death. Blue also has some intimations of mortality. Red is the favored color for celebration, happiness, starting a business, announcing a wedding, and almost everything else. In colonial government circles, however, only the governor himself was allowed to use red ink! Yellow is the color of luck and good fortune, and was the imperial color.

chapter four

MAKING FRIENDS

Hong Kong is a small region with a tight-knit community. Friends made at primary and secondary school are important throughout life, and often form part of a future professional network. In many families, siblings and cousins are a firm part of one's lifelong friendship circle. Close family friends and their children—treated much like aunties, uncles, and cousins—are equally important. These are the people who will come to your aid, offering you work after graduation, or who give support during a family crisis; they receive a level of loyalty and respect akin to a real family member. Of course, later in life, during university and at work, further friendships are formed, often around shared interests rather than a coincidental

shared personal history. For some people, naming a close friend as a godparent can include financial obligations, such as giving generous rewards and gifts at key life events—like graduating high school, going to university, and getting married—let alone in the case of a family mishap. Therefore, such an offer is an honor, but not one that should be entered into lightly.

MEETING PEOPLE

Despite their matter of fact no-frills approach to strangers, Hong Kong Chinese are in general polite and friendly, often asking you where you from almost immediately. It can be especially easy to make friends in an office environment, or through a "friend of a friend" introduction. Hongkongers like socializing in groups and are always happy to make room for one more. Many are accustomed to meeting foreigners and expatriates who need some help and guidance on how to assimilate into Hong Kong life.

It is not unusual to be invited to dine with an acquaintance or work colleague at one of Hong Kong's traditional members' clubs, such as the Hong Kong Football Club, the Hong Kong Country Club, and the Royal Hong Kong Yacht Club. While these clubs were originally formed as expatriate enclaves, many now have a majority of affluent Chinese members and are good places to meet new people: they are where members relax, exercise, socialize, entertain, network, and do business. The clubs provide high-quality international food at a reasonable price in comfortable, colonial-style settings. For members with children, there are sports facilities and games rooms, making them a much-needed resource and a great place to make friends for both children and parents.

In general, Hongkongers are known for working hard and playing hard—and their outward-looking and enquiring nature means many participate in activities and social groups (such as those on meetup.com) outside work. There are language learning and practice groups, reading clubs, hiking and cycling groups, yoga and bootcamp classes, as well as creative pursuits like pottery and poetry. Hong Kong also has a number of professional development and networking groups hosted by communal workspaces and embassies.

FRIENDSHIPS
On a deeper level, note that younger Hongkongers can be shy—even emotionally immature compared to their Western counterparts—and older or married Hong Kong Chinese may be constrained by traditional notions of what is appropriate. It is easier to break into a circle in which foreigners and locals are already mixed; otherwise, you should be willing to be the only foreigner in a circle of Hongkongers, in which case

your own curiosity and willingness to learn about their culture will be valued.

It is possible to form a friendship that extends to being invited to a family gathering—out, or even at home—particularly for festivals, during which family is important, like Mid-Fall. To refuse would be considered rude and the invitation should be taken as an honor (see pages 48–9).

A sure way to impress a local is to emulate good Chinese behavior, such as being willing to listen and learn, being humble and respectful, and by reciprocating any kindness at the appropriate time. Favors and helpfulness go a long way and won't be forgotten.

A TABLE FOR TWELVE?

Eating out is the favorite way to socialize among Hong Kong Chinese. If you're offered an invitation to join a group for dinner, it is likely that further

invitations will result from the evening. "The more the merrier" is the general rule, and there will often be ten to fourteen people sitting around a table for an office lunch or family meal. The tables in Chinese restaurants are geared to this size of party. It is customary to order as many dishes as there are participants, which gives a lot of variety, and a "lazy Susan" in the middle of the big round table ensures that everyone can reach the food and help themselves to every dish. *Dim sum* is available from early morning until lunchtime, depending on the location. A small, local spot might open as early as 5:00 a.m., attracting manual workers, whereas a smart restaurant might not open until 11:00 a.m. or 12:00 p.m. It's not uncommon for businesses or colleagues to invite a newcomer to *dim sum* for lunch. (For more on *dim sum*, see pages 111–12).

As well as Chinese restaurants, which include Cantonese food, Sichuanese food, Chiu Chow, and others, Hongkongers can choose from a wide variety of worldwide cuisines. Thai, Vietnamese, Japanese, and Korean are popular, alongside Western food, particularly Italian, French, American, and English gastropub-style food. Following the trend in city centers like Manhattan, "pop ups," in which a chef or restaurant trials a new idea or offers a special menu, are becoming popular in Hong Kong. Sometimes these events last only hours instead of weeks, attracting a large crowd and social buzz, offering a different way to meet people.

ENTERTAINING

As we have seen, it is not common for Hong Kong Chinese to entertain at home due to the size of most residences. Hosting is often done in restaurants, most of which have private function rooms or screens that can be used to reconfigure the space, or in members' clubs such as the Hong Kong Jockey Club or the Country Club.

INVITATIONS HOME

Should you be extended an invitation home for dinner, arrive on time, and leave relatively early. A suitable gift for your host would be a bottle of good whiskey or brandy, with some candy or cookies. Alternatively, a plant such as an orchid would be welcome, but remember that, for some, cut flowers are bad for *feng shui*. Whatever the gift, it should always be decoratively wrapped. Don't expect your host to open what you bring—this is regarded as greedy and impatient. Likewise, if someone gives you a present, do not open it immediately, or in their presence. Put it on one side to open later, and thank the person the next time you see them.

Often a modest host and hostess will deprecate what they have, and apologize for the food. Your job as a good guest is to praise the food, so an equilibrium is reached.

When you arrive at somebody's home, it is the custom to take your shoes off and leave them by the door, although for a dinner party your host might waive the rule. Some hosts offer a simple pair of slippers to wear inside.

If you receive a more casual invitation that does not center around a meal, this is perhaps an even greater honor, showing a relaxed attitude toward you. Bring a gift such as fresh fruit—preferably something seasonal and expensive—which the fruit stall vendor might be able to package nicely, or a package of Chinese-style cookies. Note that most Chinese do not like Western-style sweet food.

Most hosts will offer you a drink and snack regardless of the time of day. In Cantonese it is customary to ask "Have you eaten yet?" rather than "How are you?" There is a duty to feed guests and food is very important. Even if you are not hungry, it is polite to accept and eat a modest amount, even if your host does not. You will probably be invited into the living room or a more formal receiving room, but do not expect to be shown around the rest of the house, and do not overstay your welcome.

DATING

While it is usual to see Chinese couples dating one another, you will also come across mixed-race couples. However, while Chinese women often date men of other races—particularly Westerners—it is much less common to find a Hong Kong man dating a woman of another race.

Attitudes to dating will vary according to the background of the Hongkonger. Internationalized Hongkongers have a Western approach—although some may be reticent about introducing you to the family because of their parents' traditional views. If you should date a local Hongkonger, it would be wise to approach the relationship carefully and to take the time to find out what expectations your partner might have. It might also be more suitable to choose Chinese rather than Western food, and not to drink too much.

In general, it is polite for the man to pay for the first time at least. It is not unusual for those living in Hong Kong to take turns, date by date, to pay for things,

partially ensuring each other's true intentions in the relationship. Many Hongkongers "go AA," meaning to split the bill equally, so while a woman might expect a chivalrous gesture, splitting the bill brings a more casual feeling to the date.

In many ways Hong Kong women are considered "high maintenance," but the truth is that people vary greatly. Some expect chivalry—even to the point of carrying their handbag and agreeing to anything they want—while others value status. There have even been cases of dating for possessions, like a luxury handbag, a situation that has been reported in the media as it has reached underage girls.

In general, take a careful approach, especially with regard to intimacy; that is, take your cue from your partner.

chapter five

AT HOME

HOUSING

Hong Kong has changed over the past forty years from a city of poor incomers from China with a largely British civil service and a few rich merchants of all nationalities to a relatively middle-class city, with a larger number of well-off people. Along with this rise in wealth has come a great change in lifestyle.

The main transformation has come in housing. In 1970, more than a million people lived in "squatter huts"—roughly made shacks with no ownership title, no services or amenities, and no modern conveniences. Enterprising individuals ran water pipes up the steep hillsides and connected dangerously swinging electric cables to flimsy sockets, all illegal and unpaid for, but tolerated because of the huge pressure of population.

Now, apart from some old squatter areas that have been "saved" (and upgraded) due to popular demand, most of the population live in high-rise apartment blocks and have enough money to acquire the latest music and entertainment systems as well as modern kitchens and bathrooms.

But space is still at a premium. It's not uncommon to find five or six people living in an apartment that in the West would hold one or two—an apartment of 500 square feet (46,451 sq. m) might have one comfortable bedroom, while another might have up to three bedrooms of almost unuseable size! Ikea, the Swedish furnishing company, and its local imitators have prospered mightily by providing cleverly designed and versatile furniture for very small apartments. A favorite unit consists of a bunk-bed on top with a workstation underneath, incorporating drawers and lighting—just right for the ambitious young schoolchild.

The grand houses on Victoria Peak and on the south side of Hong Kong Island, and in some other neighborhoods, are for the wealthy only. Hong Kong property prices per square foot rival London and Monte Carlo. For the majority, it means living in a shared apartment, perhaps without enough rooms for each person. We have seen that it is common for elderly parents to live with one of their offspring, but it is also usual for young married couples to remain living with a parent in order to save money for the future. Apartments with more space have small rooms—usually off the kitchen—to house the domestic helper(s) somewhat separately from the family. Houses always include a space for the domestic helper. Although cats were traditionally kept to keep pests like mice and cockroaches under control, pets— particularly small dogs—are increasingly popular and are often given the run of the house.

THE FAMILY

Traditionally, the Chinese were divided into clans, each with a particular surname and an ancestral village. Daughters would marry men from other clans and move away to other villages. Sons would bring wives in from other villages. For this reason, daughters were not prized. They were often called "holes in the rice bag"—they ate, but in the end they just left the family, and had to be given money to marry. That is one of the most powerful reasons behind the traditional prejudice against female children. Although this has changed with the advent of women's equality, particularly in the marketplace, there is still a certain prejudice in favor of male children, generally among the older and less well-educated.

Demographically, Hong Kong is a developed industrial territory, having birth and death rates as low as Germany or Japan. The population continues to grow because of migration from other parts of China. Young men and women from mainland China are eager to work there, sometimes as a first step to further foreign travel.

Many couples have no children, and many have only one or two children. Factors responsible for this include cramped living conditions, full employment, and compulsory education. The population has moved from the old-style huge families with a high infant mortality rate to this modern lifestyle in just two generations.

With an ageing population, the average age in Hong Kong is forty-four, older than that of neighboring countries, and the average life expectancy is around eighty-three years. Despite the traditional value of filial piety, the biggest concern in Hong Kong now is the number of elderly people living impoverished lives with very little support from the government. Many drop below the poverty line simply because they retire and no longer receive a regular wage. If their families have no money or space to support them, or they have no children, there is little else to support them. As a result, there has been a thin but steady stream of retired people crossing to the mainland, either remaining in Shenzhen, in close proximity to Hong Kong, or to the ancestral villages they may have left as children. There has been less mobility in mainland China, and the chances are that there will still be some family members in the villages.

LIFESTYLES

In general, people in Hong Kong are busy, including the school child who wakes early and does extracurricular activities after school and often on weekends too. Many Hongkongers rise early—particularly the elderly who practice *tai chi* or go for *dim sum* at 6:00 a.m. Most offices start work between 8:30 a.m. and 9:00 a.m., but some local companies start between 9:30 a.m. and 10:00 a.m., while shops in areas like Causeway Bay and Mongkok might open at midday and close at 10:00 p.m. or 11:00 p.m.—so there are also many who stay up late and get up late. Hongkongers work hard and will socialize as much as they can, but it is not unusual to work so late that upon returning home it is time to go to bed. Chores, including grocery shopping, are often slotted in whenever possible for those without a domestic helper. Most shoppers, primarily the woman of the house, will go to the grocery store more than once a week to buy what she needs, and ideally will visit the market every day to get the freshest meat, fish, and vegetables.

Eating together is important for the Chinese, and the main family meal is in the evening. But weekends are different. Eating lunch as a family on Saturday, even with grown children, or having a family meal out on a Sunday evening, is both common and important.

The Chinese love children, and it is not unusual for a stranger to engage a parent and even a small child in conversation, often centering on the child and commenting on how cute it is. Although families are now much smaller, with usually two children at most, having a big family or a number of grandchildren is still congratulated on among friends. Both children and parents work hard in Hong Kong, so there is a duality in many families, whereby parents spend little time with their children during the week and make up for it with family outings on Sunday. Unlike in the West, most Chinese have a more relaxed approach to the occasional late night, so it's not unusual to see a young child asleep on a parent's shoulder. Likewise, you might hear a very young child cry during a late cinema performance.

Love of Children
When my part-Chinese nephew visited Hong Kong when he was two, his Chinese-looking eyes and blonde hair attracted a fuss everywhere we went, with Hongkongers even asking if they could have a photograph with him! His American father was quite shocked by the reaction, but my sister merely remarked, "I'd forgotten how much the Chinese love children."   [V.C.]

The cramped and crowded nature of Hong Kong life has resulted in a particular kind of lifestyle. For a family sharing an apartment, it might be quite normal for people not to talk intimately in front of other members of the family or involve them in their lives outside. Because there is such physical proximity, individuals preserve the privacy that enables them to keep sane by maintaining a certain mental or emotional distance. Those with jobs can choose to eat with colleagues after work or even stay in the office to stream television or play games on their office computers. Clocking out late is often commended, even if it's for a social reason. But for many families it is emotional closeness that makes the situation liveable, and activities are enjoyed together, including reaching out to extended family on the weekends.

Nearly all socializing takes place outside the home. It is normal to eat out for every meal, even breakfast, and these meals are rarely taken alone. This makes life much more interesting for the visitor—all human life is out there, on the streets, in the malls, in the parks, and in all the shops and restaurants.

It is said that a Hongkonger on his or her own will sing rather than bear the silence. Those having to be by themselves—for instance traveling to work—will almost certainly be engaged with their cell phone. Nature abhors a vacuum, and Hong Kong abhors a silence. This constant noise, which rises to a crescendo in the packed restaurants at lunchtime, can bother foreign visitors from more tranquil places. But tune it out, and you will enjoy your time amid the bustling crowds a lot more.

The open areas are popular at all times of year. Snacks are eaten on park benches and outside the small, absurdly cheap eating places known as *daai pai dong*— nowadays more difficult to find in the central districts, but still flourishing in outer suburbs and new towns. In fast-food and cheaper restaurants you will probably find fierce air-conditioning to counter the body warmth of the patrons and the high temperature of the traditional stir fries.

The average Hongkonger keeps fit by walking, whether it's walking to work—in Central, using the narrow pedestrian bridges that span the city streets in an elaborate network— or indulging in the favorite pastime, window shopping, or using the weekends to visit outlying islands or the New Territories nature trails with family, friends, and accompanying music. In the summer, the beaches are packed, lifeguards perched in watchtowers along the shoreline.

Modern fashion is similar to the West and less conservative than in previous decades. The younger fashion is as influenced by the West as it is by Japan and Korea, and Hongkongers love to combine bright colors and patterns in a way that most Westerners would not. Some of the older men and women still wear traditional Chinese clothes—a pajama suit with a high collar.

Taboos

Like other Far Easterners, the traditional Hong Kong Chinese are not a tactile people. Hugging might offend; shaking hands is acceptable but not essential. The most taboo bodily matter to be aware of is not to show the soles of one's feet to anyone.

Gambling

Gambling could reasonably be said to be the Hongkongers' favorite vice—and the reason it is carefully regulated. Horse racing at Happy Valley and Shatin is extremely popular, and the races are watched by millions on TV.

At home, a very popular game played for money, equivalent to cards, is *mahjong*. It is played with a

number of small tiles
that are collected and
discarded at great speed,
causing the cheerful
noise of plastic on
wood heard all over the
territory, in particular
during a stroll through
the fishing villages of
the outer islands, where
there is no traffic to
shatter the peace.

There is a national
lottery called the
Mark Six, somewhat similar to state lotteries in other
countries. Six numbers are chosen from a total of
forty-nine. Since it was started in 1975, the Mark Six
has contributed billions to the Government Treasury
and the Lotteries Fund, a charitable fund supporting
various causes.

NAMES

The tradition in China is that there are "a hundred
surnames." There may be a few more, but basically you
will encounter the same names over and over again.
Each surname refers to a huge extended family, or clan,
and was associated with a particular town
or village, whose members would all have had the
same surname.

The surname precedes the given names. Li Ka-shing
is Mr. Li, not Mr. Ka-shing. Immigrants to English-
speaking countries were often mistakenly called by
their given names, and didn't think to complain, so for
example, Chan Ting's family in New Zealand have now

become the Ting family, and the Chan is lost forever. It is usual for someone to be referred to by his or her surname only. Using a title is normal and polite, but the next step to informality would be to use just the surname. Chinese given names are rarely used in speech. They, and family nicknames, are felt to be private, and it would be wrong for a foreign visitor to start using a given name or nickname in the hope of showing a more informal relationship.

Surnames do not always have a resonance of meaning, but the derivation is often buried in the character. Cheung is a form of the word meaning "long," and Li or Lee "plum tree."

Most given names consist of two words, conventionally written in various ways according to taste: Ka-shing as above is generally hyphenated in Hong Kong, but mainland names are written in Pinyin (a different form of romanization), in which given names appear as one word, for example Mao Zedong rather than Mao Tse-tung.

The meaning of given names is generally known and important. Women now often have names like Yuk-bing (jade ice) or Mei-ling (very beautiful), but previously there was not much gender differentiation. Most names tend to focus on the good qualities you might wish to attract to your child, such as Ming (bright), or Yan (kindness).

Many Hong Kong Chinese choose Western names, or approximations of them. These often sound like their original names—Winnie for Wing-mei, and Mabel for Mei-yan, for example. Fashions nowadays follow American or English ones, with Kelly, Candy, and Jimmy existing alongside David and Winnie. There may not be much research into the meaning or spelling of a name, but they have some connection with the Chinese name.

Scholar, Bright, Radiant, Lovely, Happy, and Silent (a girl) obviously hope to attract the right character and may be direct translations of the Chinese names. Superman, Jesus, Janus, and Hermes invoke suitable role models. You may find Paulson, Dickson, and Lawson have fathers called Paul, Richard, and Lawrence. Then there are names that sound vaguely like the Chinese: Juicy (Juicy Tang has been spotted at a supermarket checkout), Mantis, Heman (a girl), Fatman, Elvin, Pacman, and Iceman. Yet others have fantasy names, usually taken from advertisements: Benz, Bentley, Hoover, Coffee, Apple. It is also acceptable for the Chinese to change their adopted English names, although this is usually a transition made in more youthful years, or perhaps after university.

EDUCATION

Education is taken very seriously by Hongkongers. As a largely first- or second-generation immigrant community with very few resources to back them up, they perceive their children's brains to be their fortune. So schooling is long and hard, and academic achievement admired—not for its own sake, but for the earning power it gives.

Educational content and examinations are directed by government and continue to have the British shape and style of the 1970s, although in Britain itself considerable changes have occurred since then. Education is provided free for all from the age of six to sixteen.

Early Education

Nursery schools and kindergartens take children as young as eighteen months, and they soon start the business of learning. Rhymes and elementary arithmetic start young. Chinese children seem to have an innate ability to concentrate at an early age, and it is common

to see a class of three-year-olds all looking at the teacher and not fidgeting. Modern methods have introduced much more play and activity into the classroom at this stage but traditionally this was a time for rote-learning.

Primary school starts at the age of six. Most schools have two shifts, so the school day may be from 7:30 a.m. to 1:30 p.m., or 1:00 p.m. to 5:00 p.m. Classes tend to be large. Learning to read and write Chinese must be done by rote, and takes years, as each character must be learned from scratch, and some require as many as twenty-two separate strokes of the pen. From the beginning, homework is given, and it is not unusual to hear of children at primary school working three hours a day outside class time. There is little space for play areas, so education is very sedentary even for small children.

Secondary Education

By this time, the children are accustomed to hard work and lots of homework. Even though taught in classes of forty to fifty, they outstrip most other cultures in exam achievement, and attribute this to the sheer amount of work put in, on the assumption that practice makes perfect. One girl who later went to boarding school in England said, "Here they think four math problems for homework is a lot. I am used to doing fourteen."

Most children attend government schools, but there are some important and prestigious private schools run by Christian and other charitable organizations. The fees are not high, but the intake is selective and preference is given to sons and daughters of alumni. In this way an elite has arisen in the past fifty years, and many of the top professionals and businesspeople come from it.

There are several catchment area-free international schools. The English Schools Foundation provides an English-medium education with the English curriculum and an option between the English exam system and the increasingly popular International Baccalaureate (IB). Many other international schools, including the Canadian, Singaporean, and Japanese, also offer the IB. Although these schools were started for their own nationals, many take children from other countries, including other Asian countries. Nationality may be misleading, as many students with British, Canadian, or Australian passports are in fact ethnic Chinese, their parents having emigrated to establish foreign nationality and then returned to resume making money at home.

Higher Education
Such is the demand for education that there are thirteen universities in Hong Kong. The oldest and perhaps the most prestigious is the University of Hong Kong, officially established in 1911. It occupies some gracious old buildings and a welter of new blocks to the west of Hong Kong Island.

There are also a number of specialist colleges, such as the HK Academy for Performing Arts, and private schools of commerce and language.

Those who can afford it, usually send their children overseas for tertiary education, to places like the UK, America, Canada, and Australia.

Soaring Costs

Getting a place at an international school has become a problem in Hong Kong, especially for expatriates. Those who are the child or sibling of a previous (or current) student are given priority. Many schools offer "debenture places," but gone are the days of corporations paying for their employees' children's education. The cost of such an education has soared in Hong Kong—one of Britain's top private schools, Harrow, now has an international school in Hong Kong—and has become an issue in attracting expatriates to the territory. The government has supported the opening of new international schools, sometimes by way of making land available for them, but some expatriates have reported having to home school their children for their first year in Hong Kong.

TIME OUT

HOLIDAYS

This is a hardworking culture, in which the average Hongkonger receives twelve to fifteen days of paid annual leave, though the law stipulates just seven. In addition, workers receive the statutory public holidays (see page 74). Local Hongkongers who run small family businesses, such as shops selling dried and fresh provisions, might only take leave during Chinese New Year, often closing for three to seven days. Families like these will usually stay in Hong Kong or visit relatives in China.

Some festivals include special events that are worth experiencing, even just once, like the Cheung Chau Bun Festival, the flower market in Victoria Park,

which stays open until 6:00 a.m. on the eve of Chinese New Year, or the Tai Hang Fire Dragon Dance, which takes place during the Mid-Autumn Festival.

For the average office worker, festivals allow time off that can be spent with family or friends. Eating is central to most of these occasions, and while other entertainments—going to the cinema, playing Chinese board games, singing karaoke—are popular, on most festivals the streets are empty and traffic is minimal as people remain at home together. For the visitor, such days may be eerily quiet, but with the exception of Chinese New Year, all the shops and restaurants will be open.

Time is precious for Hongkongers, so festivals are sometimes used for travel outside Hong Kong. Flights will be busy and expensive during any festival that precedes or follows a weekend, as most plan well ahead. Compared to Westerners, most Hongkongers take shorter trips abroad and dislike spending too much time away from work. It is the expatriates in Hong Kong who typically make longer trips to destinations further afield.

Festival days attract local tourists to the outlying islands of Lamma and Cheung Chau, and ferries might

even fill up before their departure time. During the summer, weekends are also occasions for visiting the outlying islands or villages in the New Territories, such as Sai Kung, which is famous for its seafood restaurants. In the winter, hiking is popular because the weather is cool and pleasant.

EATING OUT

Hongkongers are sociable people who pack their schedules year-round. It is normal to have several dinners—with friends or family—planned throughout the week, and it's not unusual to be invited along, even as a newcomer (see page 83).

Hong Kong prides itself on the huge range of cuisines available in its more than sixteen thousand restaurants catering to all budgets and tastes. In the Cantonese language there is a clear division between an informal, fast café-style outlet called a *cha chaan teng*—which serves Cantonese food and Hong Kong-style Western food such as French toast, or baked pasta dishes—and a formal or smart restaurant, which might serve both Cantonese food or any other style of food. Until thirty years ago, most locals would eat only Cantonese food at home or when out, but the internationalization of the city has caused an upsurge in the popularity of other styles of cooking and eating.

CHINESE FOOD
Cantonese
The Cantonese regard their food as the best in the world, and even other Chinese acknowledge its flavor and variety. Some say Cantonese cooking is to China what French cooking is to Europe.

Easy emigration from the New Territories in the 1960s and '70s has led to the proliferation of so-called Chinese restaurants in many parts of the world, which produce a travesty of the traditional dishes in order to please the local palates. True Cantonese cooking is as far from the *chopsuey* (an American invention that means "miscellaneous bits") and the *chowmein* of Britain or America as French cooking is from bottled sauces with French names. A very un-Chinese meal appears in Canada as "Chinese smorgasbord," and tends to consist of a buffet of dank metal tubs containing meat and vegetables cooked hours earlier.

The good Chinese cook shops twice a day to ensure the freshness of the ingredients, though frozen and convenience foods are catching on in Hong Kong as everywhere. Fresh produce markets abound, and are a vital part of any area.

The Cantonese say that they eat "everything with four legs except tables and chairs, and everything in the sky except planes," or "anything that walks, swims, crawls, or flies with its back to heaven." This all-inclusive attitude leads to some bizarre and, to Westerners, repugnant recipes, including rice worms, civet cat's paws, snails, and snakes. At home, however, the usual food is less adventurous. A meal for a family of four might consist of three courses with rice. The courses do not succeed each other as in a Western meal, but are put on the table as soon as they are cooked.

Food is for the most part cooked by stir- or deep-frying, which means that it is done quickly and should be eaten immediately, while crisp and fresh. Raw food, except for fruit, is viewed with suspicion, and salad is not on the Cantonese menu. Even lettuce and watercress are lightly fried. This is a prudent health measure, as the use of pesticides is widespread. Much of the fresh

produce comes from the mainland, although there are a number of small organic farms in Hong Kong. The market seller can tell you which items are from Hong Kong and which from China, or beyond.

A typical meal will have at least two kinds of protein, served at more or less the same time. Fish and seafood are very popular with Hongkongers, and were the staple protein of the original fishing communities, but they are more expensive today. Pork is the meat of choice—in Chinese the word meat written on a menu implies pork, while other meats are clearly specified. Beef comes second because lamb is not used in Cantonese cuisine; sheep do not thrive in the subtropical south of China, and the flavor is regarded as "too strong" and unpleasant. Poultry is well liked, with chicken being common, and duck or goose used for many popular dishes. Bean curd is another important source of protein, and strict Buddhist vegetarians make many dishes with it.

The Chinese traditionally believed that it was unseemly (and possibly dangerous) to have knives at the table, which is why everything is cut to bite size. Chopsticks are of ancient origin, long antedating the forks of Western cuisine. Once you have witnessed their expert use they will never seem awkward and limited again, but it does take time and practice to become adept. Chinese cooking therefore starts from the premise of small pieces, which makes stir-frying such an ideal method. It combines keeping as much as possible of the food's freshness and flavor with speed of preparation. For extra flavor, very strong sauces are used in sparing quantities.

The Cantonese staple is rice. Every home will have a rice cooker, a slow electric cooker where a certain amount of water is put with the rice. Once cooked, it keeps hot with a thermostatic control. Steamed or boiled rice is served with all meals. At breakfast, congee, or *juk*, may be eaten; this is a watery rice gruel flavored with stock, or cooked with chicken or fish for added flavor. Sauce, herbs, peanuts, and preserved eggs (see below) are served with the dish. Modern, busy Cantonese tend either to go out for breakfast or to grab a bowl of cereal or slice of toast like their Western counterparts.

Hundred-Year-Old Eggs

These eggs, which you will see for sale in the market or quartered on a plate in a hotel breakfast buffet, do have an ancient look to them. They are in fact only about a hundred days old. They should be duck eggs, and they are preserved in potash and salt. The white turns dark gray, and the yolk has a green to black color. They have a rich flavor, but do not taste old!

Typical dishes on the Cantonese menu include chicken or pork, stir-fried with a few vegetables such as onions, Chinese celery, or peppers; sliced beef in black bean sauce; fish steamed with ginger and spring onions; and fried bean curd and vegetables. A green vegetable is usually served as well, either fried with garlic and ginger or steamed and served with oyster sauce. Vegetarians beware—these vegetables are often cooked in meat stock.

Choi sum is the most typical Hong Kong vegetable, also known as mustard greens. *Pak choi* or *bok choi* and Chinese kale, *gaai laan*, are also popular. One of the most delicious vegetables is *dao miu*, or pea shoots, which come into season in November. Cooked vegetables often come in longer pieces, which are held in the chopsticks and nibbled.

A light broth, much like a stock, is served at every meal. Snake soup is a specialty of winter cooking, meant to help build up resistance to the cold.

Desserts were not part of ordinary Cantonese culture, but today the meal often ends with fruit.

Bird's Nest Soup

Most people think "bird's nest soup" is a fanciful name, and are incredulous when they hear that it is actually made from bird's nests. Only one type of bird, the swiftlet of Southeast Asia, makes nests suitable for this soup. The nests are made of the bird's saliva. Luckily for the swiftlets, the nests are hard to reach. Gatherers have to climb up inside dangerous caves, balancing on bamboo poles. The flavor of the soup is subtle, and it is usually accompanied by a sweet vinegar to spice it up. It is its reputation as an aphrodisiac that makes it so popular, as with many rare and unusual foods in China.

Dim Sum

Dim sum is literally translated as "touching the heart," which implies that you can eat "to your heart's content." It refers to a meal taken any time between early morning and early afternoon. Most dishes are steamed and served in bamboo steamers. In traditional restaurants, they are taken from table to table on trolleys, served by stern, middle-aged women, who shout their particular specialty's name as they pass around the room. The dishes consist mainly of three or four steamed buns, dumplings, or noodle rolls called *cheung fun* with a variety of fillings—meat and prawns as well as vegetables. Some fried foods, like spring rolls and fried buns, are also on the menu.

You can usually order green vegetables and rice dishes as well, but you do not need these to make a satisfying brunch. Tea is the standard drink, and the morning *dim sum* outing is often referred to as *yum cha*—drinking tea.

Traditionally, the price of the meal is calculated by counting the dishes left on the customer's table.

However, nowadays many *dim sum* restaurants record the dishes on a card at the table and some dishes cost more than others.

Hakka

The Hakka were latecomers to southern China, and settled in the most steep and arid areas of Guangdong and Hong Kong, a long way from the growing areas. As food could not be procured fresh twice a day, it had to be preserved, so the cuisine is not in the "just-picked" style of the Cantonese.

Two traditional Hakka recipes are salt-baked chicken, supposed to be baked inside a heap of hot salt, but often just cooked in salty water, and beef-ball soup, a clear broth with lettuce and beef balls.

Beijing

Probably the best-known Beijing dish is Beijing or Peking Duck, which consists of thin slices of roast duck wrapped with plum sauce and spring onion in a thin pancake, eaten with the fingers. Beijing cuisine contains largely wheat-based food, such as noodles and buns, which makes the northerners taller and larger than the Cantonese.

Sichuan

Western Chinese food is hot and spicy, and the Cantonese love it. *Ma po tofu*, or "old lady's bean curd"—minced pork and bean curd in a hot and tasty sauce—is a particularly popular dish.

Formal Meals and Festivals

For formal dining, such as banquets and Chinese weddings, certain dishes have ritual significance because of their names, which sound like lucky phrases. Spring dinners are often held at and around Lunar New Year, and one dish you will always find at these is moss and dried oysters. Its Cantonese name is *fut choi ho si*, which translates as "Good business in the New Year." Steamed fish, which is nearly always on the menu of a banquet, has no special name, but the word for "fish" and the word for "surplus" sound the same. Mushrooms, pork leg, and duck's feet mean "To be successful everywhere."

Special food and drink for festivals also sometimes have verbal or visual references to other things. The moon cakes cooked for the Mid-Fall or Lantern Festival, for example, contain a whole salted egg, which looks like the full moon. They are also stamped with a lucky written character.

DRINKS

With Chinese food, the universal drink is Chinese tea. This is usually served as soon as you sit down and *cha chaan teng* and *dim sum* restaurants will likely charge a small fee per person, but you can refuse the

tea and have it removed from the bill. In a *cha chaan teng*, ordinary "Chinese tea"—a cheap form of oolong—is served. In both *dim sum* and smarter restaurants you can ask for the tea of your choice. Otherwise, Jasmine tea will probably be served. When your teapot is empty, it is customary to leave the lid half open to indicate to the waiter to fill it up with hot water again. It is traditionally thought bad for the health to drink ice-cold drinks; if plain water is ordered, it will often be brought hot.

There are, of course, many different types of tea, and there are fascinating specialist shops with all the varieties on display. One that the visitor might come across is "pu erh" tea, served very strong in tiny cups, after a meal. It has the same style and kick as an espresso coffee. Jasmine tea and Chrysanthemum tea can also be ordered in most restaurants.

It is customary for waiters or for your Chinese hosts to replenish glasses or teacups from time to time, and they are traditionally thanked by tapping with the fingertips on the tabletop, so that the flow of conversation is not interrupted.

Other tea drinks include iced lemon tea, a Hong Kong institution, served sweetened or with sugar water on the side. Hong Kong-style milk tea is a strong, stewed tea served cold or hot, with evaporated milk, to the disgust of most Westerners. *Yuanyang*—a mixture of coffee and milk tea—is especially popular in *cha chaan teng*.

Most of the population worldwide has been thoroughly saturated with Coke, Sprite, and other soft fizzy drinks, and Hong Kong is no exception. There is also a taste for fresh fruit juice, the fresher the better, which you can also buy from a street-side stall. Note that most cartons of juice are filled with sweeteners and sugar.

Light beer is a cheap, pleasant, refreshing drink with or without food. The locally made San Miguel, and Tsingtao, from a northern Chinese factory started by Germans, are as popular as Heineken and Carlsberg.

At a banquet, brandy is often the drink of choice. Those who do not wish to quaff glassfuls of it are offered Sprite to dilute it with—not the most respectful way of treating a four-star drink, but acceptable to Eastern palates. At a traditional banquet so-called "Chinese wine" would be served as a digestive after the meal. This is a distillation from rice, millet, or other grains, often flavored with herbs and flowers. *Mao tai* is probably the

best-known, based on millet. It's fiery, with a strong flavor and a 70 percent alcohol content. *Siu ching* wine is yellow, with a flavor rather like dry sherry, and is often used in Cantonese cooking.

Grape-based wine and other imported drinks are freely available in Hong Kong and duty-free since 2008, making Hong Kong one of the biggest wine markets in the world. As a result, a huge variety can be found in supermarkets and specialist shops as well as most restaurants. Similarly, Western-style tea and coffee shops are highly popular, from franchised chains like Starbucks and Pacific Coffee to a range of independent cafés run by stylish, young Hongkongers.

TIPPING

The smarter hotels and restaurants add a 10 to 15 percent service charge to the bill, but some people leave an additional tip of a few HK dollars to the room staff or waiter, and this will probably go to the individual rather than into a common fund. In ordinary restaurants where no service charge is added, you can leave ten to twenty HK dollars, and polite staff will often try to return it to you or thank you profusely. In more casual coffee shops and cafés, you can check the bill to see if service has been added.

Most taxi drivers don't expect a tip, but if they owe you change they will round the fare up to the nearest HK dollar. There are standard extra charges for baggage or pets.

In general, if you have received better-than-average service, or are a regular customer, give a tip—it will be welcomed.

SHOPPING

It is something of a cliché that Hong Kong is a shoppers' paradise, but like all clichés, it is true! It used to be a place for the cheap and cheerful, but now every kind of product is available from cheap to seriously expensive. Whether you like browsing in the street markets or sauntering through the marble malls, your taste can be indulged. Winter sales (late December to February) and summer sales (July to September) are good times to shop for expensive items, as major discounts are available for the avid shopper. The Hong Kong Tourism Board is concerned that there should be good service across the spectrum of shopping experiences, and they reward local enterprises that provide it with Hong Kong Awards for Services.

The main shopping areas in Hong Kong are Central and Causeway Bay on Hong Kong Island, although Stanley market remains popular with tourists, and the length of Nathan Road and neighboring streets in Kowloon. Other areas worth exploring are Maritime Square on Tsing Yi Island near the airport, which combines old and new in two hundred shops and restaurants, and Ap Lei Chau Island just off Aberdeen, for discount furniture and clothing. All the towns have their own mini-malls, stores, and markets.

It's important to compare prices, as there is a lot of competition between stores, and you will kick yourself if you find the same item at a lower price just next door to the store you have patronized! Check also that electrical goods have international guarantees. Many stores offer a packing and postal service, with insurance, which is undoubtedly the safest and most convenient way of getting your treasures home.

Prices are often not fixed, but prolonged haggling isn't the Hong Kong style. In the cheaper markets you may get a slight discount if you buy several items, but generally they are cheap enough not to bother about. In more upmarket stores, it's worth looking dubious when you are quoted a price, and asking if they can't give you a discount or a better price. In the electronics or jewelry shops this usually works quite well. You can also use your knowledge of other shops' prices to beat them down.

Most shops are open daily, 10:00 a.m. in Central (but boutiques often open at 11:00 a.m. or 12:00 p.m.) and close any time from 8:00 p.m. onward. Supermarkets open 9:00 a.m. to 9:00 p.m or 10:00 p.m. Shops in the busy retail areas of Causeway Bay and Tsimshatsui (Tsim Sha Tsui) tend to open and close later (11:00 a.m. to as late as 11:00 p.m). Banks, Monday to Friday, 9:00 a.m. to 4:00 p.m or 5:00 p.m., Saturdays, 9:00 a.m. to 12:30 p.m.

The Malls

Hong Kong has several beautifully designed multi-storey malls, which have all you need under one roof. Pacific Place, the International Finance Centre Mall (IFC), The Landmark in Central, and Festival Walk in Kowloon are just some of these. In them you will find the famous names,

with international designers, all popular with visitors and locals alike. If you start to flag, there are stylish coffee bars and fine restaurants to restore your energy.

Department Stores

World-class department stores from many countries can be found all over the territory. In Central, Lane Crawford, Wing On, and Sincere are three locally owned stores. Among top foreign firms are Sogo and City'super from Japan, and Marks & Spencer from Britain. These have mouthwatering food halls as well as floors of fashions and housewares. Particularly good value is Yue Hwa stores, where you can find a huge range of Chinese goods.

Factory Outlets

Many expatriates have discovered the joys of factory outlets. They sell overruns and stock surplus to requirements, all good quality, as well as samples and quality control rejects that are less than perfect. Be sure to examine the goods carefully for obvious defects.

Most of the outlets specialize in women's clothes, and you can find silk, cashmere, cotton, linen, and knitwear. Apart from the very good bargains to be had, the principal reason for their popularity is that the sizes are Western and therefore more generous than the average Asian sizes. Some factories produce clothing for famous designer labels, and you usually find the labels cut out. There are a few outlets with men's and children's clothes too. Some specialize in porcelain, furniture, or candles, and it's a good plan to get the Hong Kong Tourist Board's leaflet on factory shopping. There are numerous clothing outlets in Pedder Building, Pedder Street, Central, and in Granville Road, Tsimshatsui, Kowloon. Most of the best ones are concentrated on the Kaiser Estate, a large warehouse area in Hung Hom.

Markets

There are market halls in every urban center in Hong Kong, with a variety of fresh foods, cheap clothing, and housewares. There are also several areas of street stalls, notably "The Lanes" in Central, and Jardine's Bazaar in Causeway Bay. The open-air Night Market in Yau Ma Tei and Stanley Market cater mostly to foreigners and tourists. Ladies' Market on Tung Choi Street in Mong Kok is a popular street market with cheap clothing, accessories, and housewares. There is a specialist Flower Market near Prince Edward Station in Kowloon, and the Jade Market (see below).

Art and Handicrafts
China Products, Yue Hwa, and CAC (Chinese Arts and Crafts) have a good range of Chinese art and handicrafts. Shanghai Tang is a chain store specializing in high-quality and unusual products. Hollywood Road and Cat Street in Sheung Wan is the hub of the antiques trade, where you can find silk and embroidery, porcelain, and metalwork.

Jade
The Chinese character for jade touches upon the three adjectives it represents—pure, noble, and beautiful. The Chinese have always prized jade, and the four

hundred stalls in the Jade Market in Yau Ma Tei have every type and style of jade ornament, from rings to elaborately carved Buddhas. Colors range from white to green so dark it is almost black. Top-quality jade is pure, translucent "apple" green or dark green, cold to the touch, and very expensive. Most pieces have a yellow tinge but any cloudy, gray, or brown tints are less valued. It is regarded as a protective stone, and babies are often given a jade ornament.

Tailoring
Hong Kong is famous for the speed, good value, and craftsmanship of its tailoring. There are numerous tailors, both Chinese and Indian, in the streets off Nathan Road in Tsimshatsui, Kowloon. They can make anything from silk Chinese dresses known as *cheung sam* to business suits, or a copy of one of your favorite garments.

Jewelry and Watches
High-quality jewelry and watch shops abound in Hong Kong. The prices aren't rock bottom, but the quality and variety are astounding.

Electrical and Electronic Goods
Hong Kong is gadget-crazy, and you can find many good bargains in this sector. Hundreds of stores sell cameras, household gadgets, audiovisual equipment, and computers. The Golden Computer Arcade and the Golden Shopping Centre near Sham Shui Po MTR station, as well as WanChai Computer Centre (130 Hennessy Road) and 298 Computer Zone (298 Hennessy Road), are crammed with hardware and software stores. While generally still cheaper and offering more variety than the West, the incredible bargains of yesteryear are no longer available since police crackdowns on piracy.

Optical Goods

Glasses and contact lenses are reasonably priced and can be made astonishingly quickly in Hong Kong. The optical shops stock a huge range of frames. Many of them have a resident optician who can see you right away, is very professional, and can provide you with a free prescription within minutes.

INTERNATIONAL ENTERTAINMENTS

You name it, you've got it. Hong Kong has always had more than its fair share of shows and concerts as Western players passed through on their way to elsewhere in Asia, so top orchestras, theater and dance groups, and solo artistes are no strangers to its shores. There are fifteen attractive cultural venues of varying size and capacity.

Every year there is an International Film Festival, with entries from over forty countries, and the Hong Kong Arts Festival, one of the most exciting events of its type in the Asia–Pacific region. Art Basel Hong Kong started in 2013, following on from ArtHK, which was inaugurated in 2008. Now, a number of art fairs and satellite events take place throughout the year. Pan-Asian cultural events like Legends of China and the New Vision Arts Festival are held in alternate years. Hong Kong has its own ballet and other dance companies, as well as a Philharmonic Orchestra, a Chinese Orchestra, and a Sinfonietta.

If you are more interested in places to relax, there are bars featuring live music in all the top hotels, the Fringe Club has comedy and jazz, and there are plenty of clubs with dancing and music.

International movies are popular. There are some smart modern multiplex cinemas, and most new movies reach Hong Kong very quickly.

In addition to the arts and antique galleries centered on Hollywood Road in Central, there are both public and private galleries.

Details of special events can be found at the Hong Kong Tourist Association's Web site, www.hkta.org.

CHINESE-STYLE ENTERTAINMENT

Apart from the Hong Kong Chinese Orchestra, there are several small musical groups that play Chinese music.

Cantonese opera is the most traditional homegrown entertainment, and it is worthwhile sampling it, because there is nothing like it in Western culture. There are programs throughout the year taking place in different theaters.

Cantopop, modern pop music sung in Cantonese and occasionally Mandarin, is very popular in Hong Kong, although nowadays, K-pop (Korean pop music) is considered ultra cool. There are a number of stars, many of whom also appear in Hong Kong movies, so there are often concerts.

Although the Hong Kong film industry seems to have had its heyday, Hong Kong and mainland movies are still popular with locals and are screened at cinemas with English and traditional Chinese subtitles. Hong Kong films provide an interesting insight into local culture; if you don't like violence, avoid any film about triads.

For foreign visitors eager to get a taste of Hong Kong culture, the Tourist Association also provides many tours and introductions to diverse cultural aspects of the place.

DAYS OUT AND EXCURSIONS

The city area is endlessly interesting to explore, as there is still a fascinating juxtaposition of the ultramodern and the traditional. The Tourist Association publishes leaflets of walks in and around the city. But if you are yearning for some peace, there are several ways of escaping the buzz. About 40 percent of Hong Kong's territory is Country Park, and you can find yourself with a wide view of greenery and woodland and not a single building. There are some stunningly beautiful beaches in Hong Kong, with golden sands and craggy cliffs. The waters are sometimes filled with trash, mainly bits of plastic, which come from local sources as well as the Pearl River. The government has put a lot of effort and money into cleaning the beaches and monitoring the pollution count, which is published for every beach.

Hong Kong Island

If the weather is clear, the best place to start is the Peak. This is the tallest mountain on Hong Kong Island, and is best approached by the Peak Tram (see page 132). From the top of the tram there is a level walk around the mountain, which offers views over the busy city on one side and over green slopes and the South China Sea on the other. It takes nearly two hours if you go at the leisurely pace it deserves. Part of it is a fitness trail, if you feel in need of more exercise. Tougher types can climb up from the tram to the top of the Peak, where there is an observation table and the gardens of an old governor's residence, long since burned down.

Hong Kong Park is an oasis of green in the heart of the urban landscape of Admiralty. It includes an aviary, a greenhouse, the Hong Kong Visual Arts Centre, and the Flagstaff House Museum of Tea Ware. On a near-vertical site, it is a great example of modern garden design and facilities blending with the natural landscape. Just above the park are the zoo and botanical gardens, also pleasantly green in the middle of the city. There are some interesting animals and colorful birds, and several places to sit and enjoy nature.

Ocean Park is a lively theme park with pandas, dolphin shows, and a striking aquarium, alongside a range of other visual experiences and rides. It has huge views over the South China Sea and a spectacular cable car ride across the cliffs. Hong Kong Identity

Card holders are given free entry on their birthday, but otherwise it makes for a rather expensive but very enjoyable day out for the whole family.

Aberdeen is the oldest habitation on Hong Kong Island, and is the center of a large fishing industry. Previously most of the inhabitants lived in boats in the harbor but most of these have been rehoused in the usual high-rise blocks and a smart marina has taken their place. The famous "floating restaurants" serve seafood and other Chinese dishes in Aberdeen harbor.

Repulse Bay and Stanley are two settlements on the south of the island. The ride along the road to Stanley via Repulse Bay has wonderful views. Repulse Bay has a large beach, which is kept very clean, a replica of a 1920s hotel, and a Buddhist temple next to the beach.

Stanley has one of the most popular market areas, with clothing and handicrafts available at competitive prices. Threatened with closure a few years ago, the market traders and outraged shoppers mounted such a protest that they won the day.

Shek O and Big Wave Bay are seaside villages on the west side of Hong Kong Island that have good beaches. Both can be reached by the Dragon's Back hiking trail.

Lantau Island

There are a few sights to take in on Lantau Island, incuding the giant Tian Tian Buddha at Po Lin Monastery (see page 61). One way of getting there is to take the Ngong Ping 360—which includes a long cable car ride, a gondola lift, and a village, which has been built as a recreation of the Ngong Ping area, complete with tourist-focused restaurants and tea houses.

Hong Kong Disneyland is also situated on Lantau Island, but it is geared toward mainland Chinese visitors and might be disappointing to those who have experienced larger Disney parks in the West.

For a truly authentic experience, make the trek to Tai O, one of Hong Kong's remaining stilt fishing villages. Buses leave from Mui Wo ferry terminal and the drive takes in views of Lantau and the giant Buddha. Take a short boat ride from the pier in

Tai O and you could spot one of Hong Kong's rare pink dolphins. Be warned, Tai O becomes very crowded on public holidays.

Elsewhere, in Kowloon and the New Territories, in many of the outlying islands, and in Macau, there is an enormous variety of attractive scenery and things to do and see. Find out more through the Hong Kong Tourism Board Web site.

NIGHTLIFE
There are plenty of places to go to in the evening. After a happy hour drink (typically available from 5:00 p.m. to 8:00 p.m.) and a good dinner, take a stroll around the Temple Street night market to check out the fake watches and Western-sized clothing. Extra Extra Large in Hong Kong seems to be about Medium in the West! You can even get your fortune told here. For more refreshment and entertainment, there are several

good bars—including many karaoke bars—nearby in Tsimshatsui or on the island in Lan Kwai Fong (LKF) and SoHo or Wanchai. LKF has such an astonishing variety of bars and discos that you can stagger from one to the next all night and never go to the same one twice. You may find girls wanting you to buy drinks for them in discos—but beware, they are mostly not casual pickups but professional hostesses.

If you are looking for company but don't dance, the many girlie bars of Tsimshatsui and Wanchai can provide you with an escort. Some of these bars are topless, and at all of them a hostess will join you for a pretty expensive drink—and ask for another every ten or fifteen minutes. Snacks are not free, and even if you don't eat them, you'll probably be charged. The drink prices, although posted somewhere in the bar by law, tend to escalate as the evening progresses.

Hotel coffee shops are open twenty-four hours, and there are night buses, so if you want to be out until the early hours, food and transportation aren't a problem.

SPORTS AND EXERCISE
The lack of space for fields and pitches means that few children have the chance to play much sports. Most will be taught to swim, and many play basketball— there are a large number of courts around the city— volleyball, or table tennis. Some local high schools have climbing walls. Among expatriates, or for the international school child, rugby, football, and tennis are popular options. Golf is popular, but the public courses are usually jam-packed, and the private ones are extremely expensive.

Adults take exercise either by going to a gym or by walking, including hiking in the country parks, where

there are often fitness trails. Traditionally, the Chinese get up early and go to an open area, if possible up a hill, to do *tai chi*. You may join these groups in their hypnotic exercises. They tend to attract older people who, according to statistics, remain flexible and fit and have a good life expectancy. Expatriates tend to join recreation clubs, which have swimming pools, tennis courts, and other leisure facilities.

chapter seven

TRAVEL, HEALTH, & SAFETY

ARRIVAL

Hong Kong is vibrant and noisy, and on first arrival can be both overwhelming and exciting. But it is also easy. Transportation is well organized, regular, and affordable, and signs are written in English as well as Chinese characters. Many people speak English, so if you need help it won't take long to find someone who can offer advice. As Hong Kong is such a popular destination, it is best to book at least your first night's accommodation in advance in order to avoid the hassle of finding somewhere on arrival, but it is only in peak seasons, such as during the Hong Kong Rugby Sevens in March, that accommodation can be lacking, regardless of price.

GETTING AROUND

Traveling around Hong Kong can be a delight. There is probably a greater variety of forms of transportation than in any other city. Paying for public transportation is best done by means of an Octopus Card. This is a contactless smart card that can be used on all major forms of transportation as well as in various food outlets. It will work through a bag or wallet, and so can be used with a minimum of inconvenience. The smart chip can even be put into a ring or other fashion item—

this is very popular with the locals. Tourist deals on Octopus Cards are not especially good value, especially if you buy a separate airport-to-city ticket for that express journey. You will be required to pay a deposit for the card, because tourists taking them home as keepsakes have cost the operating company too much money. If you are a regular visitor it is worth keeping the card as it will not expire. To have your deposit returned, hand in the Octopus at any customer service center inside the MTR or at the airport. Otherwise, make sure you have plenty of small change, as payment is often made by putting coins into a box on boarding or leaving, and change is not given.

Sea

Because of the fragmented nature of the terrain, ferries are used a lot. The Star Ferry, which plies between Hong Kong Island and the Kowloon Peninsula, is a famous sight, unchanged for well over a century. Each ship has a name ending in Star, and has a rounded shape and distinctive green paintwork. The fares are low, and the comfort minimal, but it is one of the best ways of viewing the harbor and the skyline, especially during the daily Symphony of Lights show at 8:00 p.m.

The outlying islands are accessed by two types of ferry, the slow, ordinary ones, and smoother, more modern craft, and the trip alone is worth it. You swoop out of the harbor past the city and see unfolding vistas of peninsulas and islands—most clad in buildings but as you get further away, just dark green with dense scrub.

Rail

There is a very good, fast Mass Transit Rail system (MTR), with ten heavy rail and twelve light rail lines, with a total of eighty-seven heavy rail stations and sixty-eight light rail stops. All these are very busy at peak times, and you can miss your stop on the MTR if you are wedged in the middle of a car. Much of the rest of the time it is the best way to travel for distances of more than about a mile, being air-conditioned, smoke-free, frequent, and very clean. In addition, through trains operate between Hong Kong and mainland China from Hung Hom Station in Kowloon.

To ascend the Peak for the first time, the Peak Tram is a must, unless you are of a nervous disposition. It is not a tram, but a cable car, and was built by a Swiss company in 1888, when it had a steam engine. It winds up from Central at a neck-twisting angle, among the skyscrapers, with panoramic views of the harbor and Kowloon.

Trams, real trams, run along the flat, northern shore of Hong Kong Island, and are probably the cheapest way of seeing the amazing city. They stop very frequently, and are the favorite method of short-distance city travel. There was a move to get rid of them in the 1970s as they were not modern enough, but fortunately they were saved and carry a lot of people who would otherwise crowd into the buses and MTR. The fare is shown inside the tram, and you put money into a box as you leave, or swipe your Octopus card. As one of the most affordable

forms of transportation in Hong Kong, they are widely used by the elderly and domestic helpers.

Road

There are bus routes all over the territory, and if you have plenty of time this is an excellent way to view street life. The fares are usually displayed both at the bus stops and inside the buses. Put the correct change in the box when you board, or use your Octopus card.

For a much faster ride, there are minibuses, which stop when flagged down. The green minibuses have a fixed route, from which they only sometimes deviate. In some areas, they stop where requested, and in others are only allowed to stop at designated bus stops. The red minibuses are less predictable in their routes, in which case knowledge of Cantonese is helpful. Like the big buses, minibuses require exact change, and some charge higher prices. Some of the red minibuses do not accept Octopus. The terminals of each line and the boxes inside the buses have the prices displayed; they change through the journey as the distance you can go gets shorter, so if you are in doubt, look questioningly at the driver.

To stop a minibus in the place you want, shout "*yow lok*!". In the amazingly condensed Chinese language it means "I want to get off!" although drivers also understand "Stop please!".

Taxis are quite good value. They are red in the urban area, a bit cheaper and green in the New Territories, and blue—and sometimes difficult to find—on Lantau. Tipping is not compulsory but is appreciated. Some taxi drivers talk, but many do not expect to. Their familiarity with English is not always great, and it may be difficult to make yourself understood, so it's a good idea to have the written Chinese version of the address you are visiting to show. However, there are usually people around who will interpret for you if you're stuck. Booking an Uber car via the Uber app is now popular in Hong Kong as an alternative way of getting around, and is the only personal car transportation that allows credit card payments. But beware, some drivers are less familiar with the roads than taxi drivers and the cars are sometimes very compact.

Car rental is not advisable unless you have to travel extensively in the New Territories. Public transportation, including taxis, is plentiful and cheap, and the roads are so congested and the one-way systems so complicated that for most visitors it would be a nightmare.

WHERE TO STAY

Almost any part of Hong Kong is suitable, but if you are only visiting for a few days it is better to stay close to the heart of things near Central, Mid-Levels, or Tsimshatsui. Tourist accommodation ranges from the expensive to the cheap, including the infamous Chungking Mansions, where backpackers can stay in windowless dorms amid curry shops and other low budget businesses.

Those in town for business may want to consider where the bulk of their appointments will take place. It seems silly to waste time traveling around, especially as businessmen favor taxis over the MTR, so if your appointments are Hongkongside, it is best to stay close. Today more and more large companies are opening offices in areas of the New Territories such as Kwun Tong, which is far from the business areas of Central, Admiralty, and Causeway Bay, so be prepared. Hongkongside is generally more expensive than Kowloon, although there are four- and five-star hotels in Tsimshatsui and Mongkok. Short-term serviced accommodation is also popular, useful both for businessmen and for those renovating their homes. There are a number of serviced apartments around Hong Kong and Kowloon, and it is quite common for companies to pay for new expatriates to live in them for the first few weeks of their stay.

HEALTH

Hong Kong has excellent healthcare, and while there are a number of hospitals and doctors offering private services, the public health system, based on the UK's NHS, is highly proficient. Gone are the days of rampant tuberculosis; even animals are rabies free! Issues like avian flu (H5N1) are usually caused by cross-border animals— live chickens are periodically banned from markets—or by the huge number of tourists passing in and out of Hong Kong on a daily basis, including by train from China. Malaria is not found in Hong Kong, and in general mosquitoes do not carry diseases—despite warning signs about Japanese encephalitis—but they will bite!

Companies provide employees with health insurance, although many offer only basic plans. As a tourist it is advisable to take out health insurance before you arrive. Hong Kong's humidity and temperature leave people exposed to everything from the common cold to skin conditions or other bacterial infections, and of course, tropical diseases. Although dehydration is rare for locals, the humidity is as high as 98 percent in the summer, and you will sweat profusely outdoors, so be sure to stay hydrated. Eat out as often as Hongkongers do and eventually you'll suffer food poisoning, too. Since the outbreak of SARS, cafés have generally cleaned themselves up, some favoring disposable cutlery—and most Hongkongers are quite phobic about germs, wearing a surgical mask when they have a cold and using hand sanitizer frequently. While it's not proven that these prevent germs from spreading, Hong Kong is a crowded territory, so it is wise to wash your hands regularly.

If you need to visit a doctor, you can choose any one you like. Hongkongers are also free to visit any general practitioner. Fees start from about HK $200 (US $25) for a consultation, and there are no catchment areas. Doctors in areas like Central may well charge up to five times more than many of those working in Causeway Bay and residential areas. Most doctors have graduated overseas and display their many certificates in their offices, although medical training in Hong Kong has a good reputation. GPs will prescribe and dispense most medicines, although a pharmacy might charge less. If you want to take your prescription out, let the doctor know.

Over-the-counter medicines are available, but if you need a pharmacist it might be better to visit a local pharmacy—some of which also sell pre-packaged Chinese medicine—because many of the personal care chain stores such as Mannings and Watsons (similar to Boots in the UK, or Walgreens in the USA) sell basic items such as painkillers, but don't have a pharmacy or a pharmacist on site, and will not dispense certain over-the-counter medicines as you might expect. Generally, there are fewer over-the-counter medicines available without prescription than in the UK, for example. There are some pharmacies in Hong Kong that will illegally dispense prescription medicines without a prescription.

Chinese Medicine

Traditional Chinese medicine, which understands the body in quite a different way from Western medicine, is highly trusted and sought after, and many Hongkongers will visit either a Chinese or a Western doctor depending on the ailment. Practitioners are not regulated in the same manner as Western doctors, although the government has a list of approved practitioners. As a visitor, it is best only to visit a Chinese doctor with someone who can both translate and clearly explain the remedy to you. There are many types of Chinese medicine, from acupuncture and bone setting to a multitude of herbs and dried products. Many treatments require repeated visits, and the herbs and dried products are also expected to be taken over a long period of time.

SAFETY

In general, Honkongers are law abiding and there is very little crime. Pickpocketing is not common, but it can happen so be careful with your belongings. By and large, you are likely to feel more relaxed and carefree than you would elsewhere. Should you leave your cell phone in a taxi, it is highly unlikely you'll see it again. File a report with the police if you are planning to claim anything through your travel insurance, but don't expect them to be interested in minor incidents such as this.

While corruption and triad activity are still present, to a lesser degree than times past (see pages 29–30), visitors generally find Hong Kong to be calm and safe, with even the noisy nightlife area of LKF seeing only the occasional outbreak of drunken discord.

chapter eight

BUSINESS BRIEFING

WHY DO BUSINESS IN HONG KONG?

The head of the Hong Kong Economic and Trade Office in Europe said in 2003 that Hong Kong people expected to have the world's freest economy, the lowest crime and corruption rates in the region, busiest container port, most popular international airport, busiest air-cargo hub, most independent judiciary, strongest legal system, and widest guaranteed freedoms.

Hong Kong's geographical position means that it is daytime there when it is night in North America and early morning in Europe. This means that firms with offices in all three places can actually work twenty-four hours on certain types of projects. This can be especially useful in the areas of financial services and communications.

HONG KONG'S ECONOMY

Hong Kong has long had a thriving free-market economy. It is a region with few natural resources, and trade—originally with Britain and China—has been its lifeblood. Ninety percent of food and all raw materials are imported. Imports and exports, including reexports, exceed GDP in dollar value. Hong Kong has retained its status as the freest economy in the world for over twenty years, according to the Heritage Foundation.

Even with the relationship with China, which is tightly controlled, it has managed to remain free with regard to its minimal regulations and low taxes.

Hong Kong always had extensive trade and investment ties with the mainland, serving as the world's window on the China trade. But since the return to Chinese rule, economic ties have become even stronger.

There was a fear that Hong Kong would lose out when China became a member of the World Trade Organization in 2001, but this does not appear to have been the case. Hong Kong is still seen by many as the gateway to China—and certainly the safest—despite the opening up of China and the fact that it has become easier for foreign businesses to invest and trade there. Many manufacturing centers have moved to the mainland,  where labor and production costs are lower, but typically the head offices remain in Hong Kong, mainly because of the rule of law. However, manufacturing is dwindling in the current economic climate, and has given way to services, with financial services being a particularly strong sector.

In 2003, the economy was adversely affected by SARS, a virus that killed three hundred people in Hong Kong and several thousand more worldwide. Warnings about SARS brought Hong Kong's tourism and aviation industries to a standstill. Unemployment suddenly rocketed, reaching a record high of 8.7 percent. The real estate market, which had already plummeted after 1997, crashed further. However, the economy made a strong recovery, with the value of property and goods exceeding 2003 prices. The most significant areas of growth continue to be foreign trade and tourism.

The Closer Economic Partnership Arrangement (CEPA) with the mainland government, signed in June 2003, gives Hong Kong distinct advantages over foreign competitors. China has increasingly relaxed travel restrictions between the mainland and Hong Kong, and mainland tourists have become the economy's single largest source of growth.

The 2013 Belt and Road initiative (also known as One Belt, One Road and the Silk Road Economic Belt) is driven by the People's Republic of China in order to connect and cooperate with Eurasia. Chinese leader Xi Jinping promised to create a development fund of US $40 billion, which would be used to invest in—and not fund—projects. Hong Kong has an important role in the initiative, which straddles a number of industries, including the legal sector, and many companies are doing their best to make the most of both funding and interest in the initiative to boost business.

BEFORE YOU START

Hong Kong is all about business, and business is the language most of Hong Kong speaks. Because of this, life is made easy for businesspeople, from the hotels with great business facilities, to cheap and effective communications technology, to restaurants close to or in office blocks specializing in catering to the hungry negotiator. However, there are a number of pitfalls in negotiating with Hong Kong Chinese businesspeople that you should be aware of. Don't let the superficially Western style fool you into believing that Hongkongers will act and react as Westerners do.

Do remember that, although Chinese businesspeople are eager to acquire Western technology and products, they are inherently biased against foreigners. If they can do business with a Chinese person, they will. The next best thing to being Chinese is, however, to behave as much like them as you can.

Business Hours
Hong Kong businesses work Monday through Friday, and many work on Saturday mornings as well, although the government has tried to phase this out by example, ending the requirement for civil service employees to do so. Generally, the business day starts at 9:00 a.m., but breakfast meetings are not uncommon. Lunches are sometimes long, and may start at 12 noon. Most businesses close officially at 6:00 p.m., although those in finance tend to have a shorter, eight-hour day. The truth is, nearly all staff often stay later. Bear in mind that Chinese New Year and many other holidays are bad times to try to see people, as many of them will be taking time off.

Appointments
Appointments should be made as far in advance as possible, and should be attended scrupulously on time. It is better to be early for an appointment than late, so leave plenty of time and allow for traffic congestion on the roads and even on the sidewalks. If you are late, you should apologize profusely, even if it was unavoidable, as it is regarded as very disrespectful. Be generous and gracious to anyone else who is late.

Who's Who?

Endeavor to become aware of the positions, status, and family relationship of each member of the Hong Kong negotiating team. Most businesses are small and family-owned. Even larger businesses will employ members of the same family. Age is still respected, so an older family member may well be present as a figurehead at the meeting. So it's often not appropriate to address all conversation and presentations to the senior negotiator. He or she may be a ceremonial figure, and the more junior staff will be expected to filter the relevant information to him or her.

However democratic you wish to be, paying close attention to the hierarchy is essential. It would not be appropriate to listen attentively to a secretary or to interrupt an older person. Greeting junior staff, and courtesies such as "please" and "thank you" are always welcome, but overfamiliarity will make it difficult to maintain your authority. Beware of delegating tasks of any kind, since asking employees to do something that they regard as beneath them, or outside their domain, is a breach of protocol. An inappropriate request will be quietly ignored, since it would not be right for an employee to react with indignation.

Names

Again, formality is the keynote in addressing business counterparts. In Chinese names, the surname comes first, so it would be appropriate to call Liu Kam-fai "Mr. Liu." Often a Chinese will take a Western name as well. You may see a name written thus: "Stephen LIU Kam-fai." Most married women keep their maiden names, but sometimes will write both maiden and married names: "Grace MA CHAK Ka-lei." This can be puzzling to foreigners, but in this case it would be fine to call her

Ms. or Miss Ma. It is not wrong to address a married woman as Miss, since she keeps her maiden name. In China it was customary to use Madam before a woman's surname, but this is a little old-fashioned now. Titles, like Professor and Doctor, are important to their holders.

When you know someone well, they may ask you to call them by their surname only, or by a Western name like Stephen. They may refer to their colleagues by their surnames only.

Business Cards

Business cards are an essential part of Hong Kong life, so make sure you have some printed when you are there and before you make contact. It is traditional to have English on one side and Chinese on the other although if you are ethnically Chinese and have a Chinese name, you might then be expected to speak Chinese throughout your meetings. Your card should include your title and name, the name and address of your company, and your contact telephone numbers. A Web site is also common. Most cards feature the logo of the company as well. Because the "chop," or seal, of a person or a business has always had prominence in Chinese culture, the logo has now replaced it as a symbol of the firm and it may be more memorable than a name. It is an intrinsic part of the company's identity.

You will need to have your surname (at least) transliterated into Chinese characters. This is a guide to pronunciation, although it may sound very different from your idea of your surname. Because Chinese surnames are one syllable, the first syllable of your name will be what you are addressed as. For example, Mrs. McFarlane would be "Mrs. Mak," Mr. Williamson would be "Mr. Wai," Dr. Hurworth, "Dr. Ho," and so on. You should be able to ask a trustworthy colleague to help find an appropriate name, and if you develop a three-character Chinese name, it should also have a good meaning and does not need to be entirely phonetic.

Getting It Right

It is important that the person who chooses your transliteration is scholarly enough to do it well. A slip-up in a character can result in something ridiculous, unlucky, or rude. Someone whose name was transliterated to (Wai) Ka-si found to his consternation that the characters printed meant "furniture" instead of the lofty intended meaning, "encourager of thought."

The exchange of business cards is an important preliminary ritual in Hong Kong. If someone presents you with theirs, and you do not offer one in return, they will feel that you are not interested in the acquaintance, or that you are not important enough for them to deal with. Business cards are presented and received with two hands. This gives face to both parties. It would be very disrespectful to take a card with just one hand, and if you offer one in this way, you are thought to be dismissive of your own company. When receiving someone's card, make a show of examining it for a few moments; then carefully place it into your card case or on the table in front of you.

What to Wear

Hong Kong businesspeople are quite conservative in dress. Men wear dark suits with shirts and ties in relatively sober shades, and women in senior positions tend to wear dark or subdued colors, conservative necklines, and long sleeves. Skirts of a decorous length and trousers are equally acceptable. You cannot go wrong if you imitate this style. Expatriates do sometimes wear brighter colors, particularly the now-popular pink dress shirt, or those with floral linings on the cuffs and collars, popular among Brits.

Gift Giving

It is customary to bring a gift to your Hong Kong counterparts. The type and style of the gift should be considered carefully, and it should be attractively wrapped. It is considered rude not to wrap a gift. Acceptable gifts include specialties from your home country, handicrafts, and coffee table books. You can expect to receive a gift in return. Hosting a banquet (see below) counts as a gift, and if your Hong Kong hosts do this for you, it is appropriate to host one for them, even if this occurs later on a reciprocal visit to your country. In the fairly unlikely event of being invited to a Hongkonger's home, you should take a wrapped bottle of Scotch, Japanese whiskey, or brandy, and some nicely presented fruit, cookies, or candy.

More important are the no-nos: clocks are an intimation of mortality; green hats are marks of a cuckold; blue wrapping paper is not favored because blue is associated with death.

As with business cards, gifts should be given and received with two hands. It is not considered polite to unwrap a gift in front of the giver, as it would mark you as impatient and greedy. Thank the giver, and put it to one side to be opened later.

At Chinese New Year if you happen to be in Hong Kong, it would be fitting to distribute *lai see* to unmarried junior staff who know you and have helped you (see page 76). Chinese New Year cards (or e-mails) and sometimes Christmas cards, too, will be sent to all contacts, and will be expected in return.

DIPLOMACY

Don't go straight into business talk when you first meet your contacts. Try to get to know your counterparts and create a calm, relaxed mood. A little polite conversation on a neutral topic is always a good bet. Keep off politics, Chinese politics in particular. Food is to the Chinese what the weather is to the English. Praise for local cuisine will be appreciated (but it may be a good idea to find out if your contact is Cantonese first) and some interested questions about health, festivals, or the races, but personal lives and plans are off-limits until you know someone pretty well.

Although accustomed to Western openness and frankness, many Chinese prefer to be circumspect, and will appreciate it if you are too. Don't attempt a hard sell or other aggressive moves. Direct questions may elicit less information than hints or indirect approaches. In particular, do not come out with any awkward or unpleasant facts in public—reserve this sort of frankness for private conversation. It is important to preserve someone's status in front of their staff.

Face

Understanding the concept of "face" is essential to succeeding in Hong Kong's business culture (see page 51). Showing anger and annoyance is not productive in business or social meetings with the Chinese. It actually puts you at a disadvantage because it shows a lack of control. And, since your counterpart wishes to save face, he will not want to be associated with your lack of it. You will lose a lot of points if you lose your temper. Speak calmly and present your arguments and materials in a positive and modest way. Conflict should never be apparent. Modesty is prized, as opposed to the Western idea of selling yourself.

Ways of Thinking

Western-trained businesspeople may well be logical thinkers, guided by objective and even abstract factors. This will be true of Hongkongers with further education and more experience abroad. But the majority of Chinese in business are associative thinkers. They tend to go on "feel" and "hunch" rather than facts and figures. Their faith in the philosophy of a particular company or group will probably be a central factor in their thinking. There is emphasis on the whole rather than the individual, harmony rather than fragmentation.

BUSINESS ENTERTAINING

If you meet wealthy people or those from a large company, they may have other means of entertaining you at their disposal. One big perk is the junk— a motorboat with a wooden superstructure holding up to forty people—or even a yacht. Trips are usually made on weekends to outlying islands, where drinks and lunch are served at anchor, or you might visit a seafood restaurant. Swimming and sometimes other water sports are available. You may also be invited in the evening to take a junk trip to an island famous for its seafood restaurants. It's a very pleasant way of getting out of the city, and on a warm evening you will have a beautiful view of the city lights.

Another organized outing might be to the races. Horse racing is something of an institution in Hong Kong. Everyone seems to go, although children are not allowed. The tracks are flat, and the races short, but the amount of money gambled can be phenomenal.

The lower reaches of the stadia (there are two, one in Happy Valley and one in Sha Tin) house a pushing, noisy crowd and several flourishing food and drink stalls. The upper reaches, where business bigwigs might have a "box," are very different. Each box is in fact a suite of rooms with a private viewing terrace, and superb catering. If you are enjoying your meal so much that you do not want to get up to go to the viewing terrace, you only have to turn your head to see one of the special televisions installed for the purpose. If you step outside the box, you can place bets with calm, uniformed women reminiscent of bank tellers. A poker face is necessary in Chinese society. Whether you win or lose, it is prudent to remain passive.

Another outing might involve a cultural show, for example Cantonese opera, although this is an acquired taste, lasting for four hours or more, so not many Chinese would expect Westerners to appreciate it.

THE BANQUET

The word "banquet" means something quite specific to the Chinese. Banquets are reserved for large company celebrations, such as a business deal or the annual dinner, and also for Chinese weddings. It is a formal Chinese dinner, sometimes for one table but very often for several, hosted by one person or a company. The menu is planned in advance, and copies of it will appear on each table so the guests can pace themselves. Normally, twelve or fourteen courses are served, following a certain order, although individual dishes may vary. Nearly every dish contains protein, so at one banquet you may have as many as twelve different types of meat, poultry, and fish. Usually, a dish is served into individual bowls or small plates, and presented to each guest, but items such as duck—for which it is customary to show the head and prove that a whole duck has been provided—a larger plate will be set on the table. When each course is ready to be eaten, it is usual to drink a toast to it. Watch everyone else and try to imitate them. Hold your glass up in your right hand and support it at the bottom with the left, and make a circular gesture around the table, making eye contact where possible. Then take a sip—whether it be tea, soda, beer, or brandy. Then pick up your chopsticks when your host does, and enjoy the food.

First comes a dish of cold cuts, sometimes with a few salad vegetables. After this, dishes such as whole steamed garoupa (grouper) or bird's nest soup will appear, one by one. Shark's fin is still served in many restaurants, although some restaurants and corporations have banned the serving of it. Sometimes an honored guest will be given a choice morsel by the host, and needless to say it should be received with thanks and eaten with pleasure. This can be difficult if the dish is unfamiliar, such as chicken's feet with pork fat, but an attempt should be made to eat some of it. Traditionally, you should leave something in your bowl so that you do not look greedy—or hungry—for more, but take your cue from your fellow diners.

A banquet shows how wealthy the host is, so rice and noodles are served only at the very end, in case anyone is still hungry. It is quite polite to leave these; in fact it would be impolite to finish your bowl, which would imply you have not been well enough fed.

The very last course may be a sweet dessert, and fruit is often served afterward. This signals the end of the banquet, and the hosts will get up after they've had their fruit. When your hosts go, you must too. The hosts will stand at the exit and guests thank them, by putting their hands together and bowing slightly, or by shaking the right hand of the host with both hands and bowing.

Chopsticks

Using chopsticks is an art that it is worthwhile to acquire. Hold the top third of the chopstick, like a pencil. Then fit the second stick in between the third and fourth fingers and manipulate this in a pincer movement to pick up the food. This is comparatively easy with pieces of meat or a leafy vegetable, but peanuts and similarly smooth, round objects present quite a challenge. Since SARS, it has become common for smart restaurants to put two pairs of differently colored chopsticks at each place setting. One is to serve yourself—or the guest sitting next to you might politely serve you, as a foreigner—and the other is to eat with. Chopsticks with a silver tip are traditional—the silver tip is for serving and then the chopsticks are turned around for eating—but it is common to be given two pairs. Try not to mix them up, as many Hongkongers are quite phobic about germs. Note that if you are not being served by a waiter, taking food from the center of the table with your chopsticks and putting it directly into your mouth is impolite. It should be put into your bowl first, usually with a spoon or serving chopsticks.

At elaborate or charity banquets, small but expensive gifts are put in each place, and at company banquets there are very often lucky draws for presents—you may have been given a ticket with a winning number. This all gives face to the hosts, who are seen as generous, and puts you in their debt to some extent.

Games

A large business banquet and even weddings will often have a games room just next to the banquet room. Guests can play Chinese games such as dice, card games like Chinese Poker or Deuces, nicknamed "big two" after the Chinese name *chor dai di*, which literally means "get rid of 2," and *mahjong*, a four-player game using 144 mahjong tiles engraved with characters and symbols (see pages 97–8).

Karaoke

Karaoke after a banquet is also a great favorite in Hong Kong. Before the days of karaoke, only the most intrepid or inebriated guests would take the floor and sing unaccompanied, but now nobody has an excuse not to sing along. Some foreigners feel they just cannot join in with this form of entertainment, but others love it. Your standing will rise considerably if you take the plunge! If the banquet has gone well, then the lubricants will have taken over and most barriers broken down. It's important that locals start the singing, as foreigners will often follow—even for just one effort. A bonus is to get the foreigner singing a duet with his/her counterpart. As a rule, have a go.

For the serious *aficionados* of karaoke, there are numerous karaoke bars in Hong Kong, ranging from the seedy to the opulent.

Suzie Wong

Foreign visitors are often fascinated by the world of Suzie Wong—the readily available and submissive young Asian beauty— and think the Orient should provide a mystique interlinked with sexual entertainment. However, the Vietnam days of "R & R" have been replaced by the age of AIDS awareness. Your business colleagues will not send any "live entertainment" to your hotel room unless you have expressed a wish for it, though you should be on the lookout for a subtle hint from a local who is trying to gauge your wishes.

NEGOTIATIONS

It is advantageous to keep the same team throughout the negotiations. That way, a feeling of trust and respect can be fostered. And since age is revered, it helps a lot if your chief negotiator is in his or her fifties.

It is a good plan to have several alternative options, in order to give your Chinese counterparts room to maneuver. They can then retain face while rejecting or altering some of your suggestions.

Don't assume that "yes" means agreement. It is used as a marker to show that the listener has understood what you are saying. Likewise, if you don't hear the word "no," it doesn't mean that there has not been agreement. "Yes" is sometimes offered as a polite way of masking problems or delays, so be sure to explore a topic if you feel that the answer is unclear. The Chinese will not use "no" directly, but will use a phrase such as "I'll think about it," or "perhaps." To say "no" can cause a party to lose face, particularly if you are the client, so you might need to read between the lines.

Negotiations can be very slow and protracted, with extensive attention to detail. Another point to note is that the Chinese negotiating team may request a large discount toward the end of the negotiations, which may be referred to as a "compromise," so factor this in before you start. There are also many issues that can be resolved by respecting your Chinese counterparts' belief in *feng shui* (see pages 65–9).

TEA

Don't underestimate its importance! You should always accept an offer of a cup of tea, as it shows a willingness to participate in the negotiations. When you are served, wait for the host to drink first. Teacups are useful visual aids; your cup may represent your company, for example, and the position of the cups may indicate the closeness of the two companies to an agreement.

THE RULE OF LAW

The rule of law is extremely important. It provides clarity and certainty so that people can plan their lives—you know what the law is and know that any changes to it will be made with due process. All Hong Kong government decisions are made in accordance with checks and balances, so executives cannot abuse their power, and government and its decision-making process are transparent. The police are also subject to the law and do not abuse their powers. Individuals are guaranteed a fair, unbiased hearing and trial. The rule of law is the best alternative to the rule of the whim of whomever is in power, whether it be a dictator or the tyranny of the majority. The consequence in modern liberal democracies is that basic human rights are respected.

Since the handover to China, Hong Kong's freedoms have been guaranteed by the Basic Law, which promises "one country, two systems," so the previous capitalist system and way of life should remain unchanged for fifty years. One of the main reasons for business staying in Hong Kong instead of moving into the mainland is the rule of law, which has always played a vital role in Hong Kong's success, and will continue to be essential for its future. Any tampering with or "reinterpretation" of the Basic Law might jeopardize this, which is why the Hong Kong lawmakers are so vigilant. To quote Elsie Leung, the former Secretary for Justice, "The rule of law begins with individuals and their right to seek the protection of the courts, in which justice is administered by impartial judges. It protects the freedom of individuals to manage their affairs without fear of arbitrary interference by the Government or the improper influence of the rich and powerful. Its starting point is the individual but it encompasses the whole of society."

Hong Kong has had British common law since the beginning, although certain ordinances make provision for traditional Chinese law as well. Particularly valued are the law of contract and intellectual property law, so important in the world of business. There are numerous large international and local law firms in Hong Kong, with long experience in dealing with other Asian countries. The legal system has a Court of Final Appeal (CFA), established at the handover, which is the ultimate arbiter of the exercise of common law in Hong Kong.

BUSINESS AND GOVERNMENT

The Hong Kong SAR government actively supports business, and there are Economic and Trade Offices in eleven overseas locations that can provide a great deal of information before you arrive in the territory. The government is small and efficient, and is well known for its transparency and fairness. It rarely interferes in the business community, and both personal and corporate taxes are comparatively low and simple to calculate.

The Department of Trade and Industry offers a free service to people wishing to set up businesses, providing information on all government licenses, permits, certificates, and approvals relevant to business operation in Hong Kong. The Labour Department can give information on recruitment and human resource management, the Immigration Department on visas. Help with financing is available, and once your business is launched, you can get help with development and management. Investment visas, including for entrepreneurs, are available in Hong Kong and less difficult to obtain than in countries like the USA or UK.

TRADE FAIRS

Hong Kong's Trade Development Council organizes a great many trade fairs during the year. The venue, the Hong Kong Convention and Exhibition Centre, is beautifully located on the harborside, and is a large and well-appointed building. The AsiaWorld-Expo, situated close to the airport, also boasts 70,000 square meters of event and exhibition space.

The TDC also has a range of helpful links and a Web site to enable businessmen from abroad to make contact with Hong Kong companies, listing over forty categories of goods and services. The online magazine *Hong Kong Means Business* includes a wealth of information on all kinds of Hong Kong businesses and initiatives, particularly CEPA and the Belt and Road initiative.

COMMUNICATING

CANTONESE AND MANDARIN

As we have seen, Hongkongers speak Cantonese rather than Mandarin, or *Putonghua*. They also read and write traditional Chinese characters, unlike the mainland, which uses a simplified version of these (see page 20).

Mandarin is widely taught and is compulsory in some schools. It is considered important in both impressing the mainland government and in continuing a strong business relationship with China, although some worry about the preservation of Cantonese culture.

Cantonese, like all forms of Chinese, is a tonal language, which uses nine tones. (There are four tones in Mandarin.) The six main tones, however, are enough to sound proficient, and those learning Cantonese will often only be taught those. In tonal languages a variation in the pitch of the voice conveys differences in meaning. It is difficult for the foreign ear to pick out the different tones, but over time and with practice they become easier to hear and use. Of course, when in doubt, the context of the sentence helps in understanding the correct meaning. The six main tones in Cantonese are:

- high level or high falling (1)
- mid rising (2)
- mid level (3)
- low falling (4)
- low rising (5)
- low level (6)

Emphasis is provided by additional words, usually "particles" used at the end of sentences. As a general rule, less-educated speakers emphasize particles more and, since many of these end in "—*aa*" (*aa1*) and "—*laa*" (*laa1*), there is a sound that is uniquely Cantonese.

If you get the tones wrong, a Cantonese speaker might not understand you. The words will either be meaningless or mean something completely different, which can be very embarrassing— although those more used to dealing with foreigners might well get the gist.

Hong Kong uses the Jyutping Romanization system for Cantonese, developed by the Linguistic Society of Hong Kong, an academic group, in 1993. This indicates both the phonetic pronunciation and the tone, represented as a figure. For instance, *hoeng1 gong2* (Hong Kong) indicates that "*hoeng1*" should be pronounced with the first tone and "*gong2*" should be pronounced with the second tone.

GETTING BY IN ENGLISH

Visitors can usually get by with English, although the education system emphasizes written English over spoken. It may be useful to write down names or questions if your speech is met with incomprehension. A few words of Cantonese will elicit gasps of surprise and lavish praise from the locals. With older speakers, after a couple of phrases, the praise tends to die away. There is a slight suspicion of anyone who speaks the language too well—they might understand too much!

Even when English can be used there may be difficulties. There is a confusing tendency arising from the fact that in Chinese the answer to any statement is an affirmation or contradiction of the statement. Take, for example, "You don't mean that, do you?" The answer

"Yes" would mean, for them, "Yes, you are right, I don't mean that" where English speakers would mean "Yes, I do mean that." So beware of yes and no!

Intonation is taught in English classes, but only advanced speakers get it right. So be prepared to ask for several repetitions, or for something to be written down.

Hong Kong people like to talk and will do their best to communicate, although there seems to be less willingness among the young, schooled after the handover, many of whom are awkward and lacking in confidence, sometimes despite their evident ability, and who will avoid speaking English at all. The accent tends to be strong, however, and it is sometimes difficult for a foreigner to distinguish what is being said. Bear in mind that Cantonese is a language of single syllables, most of which end in a vowel or a "stopped" vowel (like a glottal stop—imagine a London cockney saying "lot," "book," "rap," where the final consonant is not released). Hence English words ending with several consonants may well be rendered with only a passing nod to those required. Here are some common words that might fool a foreigner, where * stands for a glottal stop:

The word "Don't." *Do* shu* the door* sounds like "Do shut the door." "How old are you?" said as "*How o* you?*" sounds like "How are you?" The word "help," said as *hel**, sounds like "hell" (but receptionists seem to be taught to compensate by saying, *Can I help-t-you?*). "Drink(s)" sounds like *dring* (*What you wan* dring?*)

In the local version of Cantonese, "n" and "l" are interchanged with the "l" sound being a lazier format, so the same is expected of English—*pho lumber* (phone number); "*I do* lo*" (I don't know). Only well-practised Hongkongers can pronounce "v" sounds, which is usually substituted with "w": Wickie instead of Vickie. An "r" sound is often substituted the same way—"weally?" instead of "really?" They find a final "r" or "l" sound difficult to pronounce, and many are taught to add an "o" sound—but not later taught to remove it—resulting in "ar-o" and "el-o" when spelling words out. Likewise final "s" or "sh" on a word may be pronounced with an *ee* sound afterward, which gave rise to the "joke Chinese" style of *washee clozee* for "wash clothes."

Such well used phrases have given rise to "Chinglish," the combination of the two languages, which represents how many Hongkongers speak English. Hongkongers will often elongate words they want to emphasize, as is done in Cantonese, such as "it's sooo hot"—which would be pronounced "hooo yit." Stay long enough and you will find yourself speaking Chinglish too! In Chinese, there is no differentiation between he and she, so you can expect locals speaking English to confuse the two, regardless of how fluent their English is.

HUMOR

Cantonese is rich in slang and jokes and puns that go in and out of fashion, making it a playful, nuanced, and ever-changing language. In everyday usage in Cantonese swearing and lewdness is quite acceptable among peers. But when speaking to you in English Hongkongers will be more circumspect and modest, even though they will still be friendly and informal. Among friends, teasing can be a sign of affection and is not done to be hurtful; many love giving each other awkward (and sometimes "cute") nicknames, which can take time to shake off. Remember that jokes in English don't always translate well. Many things are phrased differently in Chinese, and in some cases the Chinese word is more specific than the English. Sarcasm is not common; teasing is more likely.

Laughter

Laughing can be misinterpreted by Westerners. Even if you are imparting serious news, such as the death of a family member, someone may laugh. It is not at all intended disrespectfully, but is a way of covering up their awkwardness. If you fall over in the street, people are liable to laugh rather than help you up, which can be hurtful and puzzling. Women often cover their mouths when laughing, as a slightly embarrassed gesture.

BODY LANGUAGE

The Chinese don't touch each other as much as Westerners now do. Shaking hands is universal, and with friends both hands may be used and the handshake may last longer. The emphasis is on dignified and courteous behavior. Slouching is regarded as rude.

A shake of the head means "no," and a nod means "yes." However, a nod may just signify understanding rather than agreement. A slight bow of the head is appropriate when being introduced to someone, or from an inferior to a superior. As congratulations or thanks, or to greet someone at New Year or some other festival, it is normal to clasp their hands and give a slight bow.

To beckon, raise your hand, palm down, and move your fingers and hand toward you.

To thank someone for pouring a drink, drum your fingers a few times on the table, to express gratitude.

Thumbs up and thumbs down—as in the West.

Cover your mouth when using a toothpick. It used to be thought unseemly for women to be seen with their mouths open and their teeth showing.

Pointing directly can be regarded as disrespectful. Another rude gesture that should be avoided is sticking your thumb between your index and middle fingers.

You may notice some Chinese people becoming red in the face after a drink. This is because the enzymes in their bodies are not adapted to breaking down alcohol, and it has a more poisonous effect on their physiology. Many Chinese women swear off alcohol altogether, as they do not like this effect.

THE MEDIA

The Chinese-language press has a huge readership, even though the racing pages may be of prime interest. The most influential papers are *Ming Pao*, the *Apple Daily*, and the *Oriental Daily*. The stance of the first two is more understanding of, than critical of, Beijing. However, a *Ming Pao* editor was controversially sacked after publishing a critical piece about local politicians. The *Apple Daily*, originally forthright in its quest for truth and exposure of scandal, has become popular for its gossipy, brash, and sensationalist tabloid style.

There are two main English-language newspapers. the *South China Morning Post* was recently bought by the Alibaba Group, a giant e-commerce company from mainland China, which many feel has led to more biased reporting. For them that leaves *The Standard*, a free newspaper, as the next-best thing. The former *HK Magazine* as well as the current *CNN Travel* and *Time Out Hong Kong* all have useful information online. There are also a number of blogs, some of which specifically cater to the expatriate or Western visitor.

There are nine commercial free-to-air television channels, with "Pearl" the only channel offering English programming that includes entertainment. RTHK is the government company that produces news and public information programs for both television and radio. It currently has three trial channels, with only the simulcast of China's CCTV-9 airing in English. ViuTV is a relative newcomer to free-to-air television. It's run by HKTVE, and operated by PCCW, Hong Kong's primary fixed-line, broadband, and cable television operator. More channels, including English-language content-driven channels, are due to be launched. Traditionally, English channels stick mainly to finance, lifestyle, wildlife programs, and dramas and movies, with news in English and Mandarin. There is a notable lack of English-language television news reporting, particularly when it comes to live issues such as the 2014 Umbrella Revolution.

Cable TV is available, offering a range of English and Chinese channels covering all categories from entertainment, drama and movies, to sports and finance. Netflix launched in Hong Kong in 2016.

Hong Kong people understand that the press is generally self-censoring—a situation that seems to have worsened in recent years. They tend to look outside the territory for unbiased reporting, particularly online. The BBC World Service, CNN, and Al Jazeera are all available on cable, as well as Bloomberg.

SERVICES
Phone Booths
Most public phones have disappeared, but they can still be found at the airport, Star Ferry, and other ferry terminals. You can usually use a phone in a luxury shop or information point at a mall, or any hotel lobby. Local fixed-line calls to other fixed-line phones, except pay phones, are free. For international calls, phone cards are readily available, for example in 7/11 stores. Some local cell phone networks offer great packages on calling abroad, so buying a SIM card is an option.

Cell Phones

It is easy to purchase a local SIM card, either at a mobile service provider's shop or even at larger 7/11 stores. SIM card packages usually include options such as just local calls (airtime), airtime plus data, or those with low international call rates or international minutes included. If you need to purchase a cheap handset in order to use a local SIM, you can easily do so in most electrical stores or computer centers. But you might just as well go to the computer center to have your cell phone unlocked. Those bought in Hong Kong are never locked to a network. Dual SIM card phones are also common, where many move between China and Hong Kong frequently. When visiting areas like the New Territories and locations close to the border, beware of data roaming as you may pick up a China network and not realize it.

Internet

Hong Kong has some of the best and fastest Internet in the world, and there are many cafés, restaurants, malls, and shops that offer free Wi-Fi. Hong Kong International Airport also offers a fantastic free Wi-Fi service. Many such places require you to agree to terms and conditions or "sign in" without giving any personal information, and will time out after one hour. Simply "sign in" again for further use.

Mail and Courier Services

Hong Kong's mail services are usually cheap, quick, and efficient. Letters take between three and five days to or from the USA and Europe. The General Post Office is close to the Star Ferry, and is even open on Sundays, which is useful for domestic helpers. Post offices and their opening hours can easily be found online.

Opening hours are typically Monday to Friday, 9:30 a.m. to 5:00 p.m., and Saturday, 9:30 a.m. to 1:00 p.m.

Major courier services as well as several local ones are available, and will pick up from almost anywhere in the city. Many MTR stations have DHL branches.

CONCLUSION

Hong Kong is probably the most extraordinary few square miles on the planet in terms of human achievement in the past sixty years. It is both exceptional and diverse. Visitors marvel at its breathtaking location, amazing buildings, exciting shopping, and fine dining. And yet you'll find opposites side by side: order juxtaposed with chaos; courteous etiquette and abrupt manners; and rich and poor living in close proximity, constantly crossing paths. Business visitors will find not only businesspeople but also the government and banks approachable and cooperative. A humble attitude and willingness to work hard is apparent everywhere, and, while it seems as though money is the main driver in this international city, people are motivated by more than the need to survive. They are driven to change their personal circumstances, and to surpass the previous generation's successes. Take the time to familiarize yourself with the city and its people and you will find a helpful attitude, a readiness to share information and provide help, and a sense of loyalty that will make you feel at ease about pursuing your own goals. Hongkongers are inventive, dynamic, and sociable people, and you may well end up making friends along the way.

Further Reading

Travel Guides

Chen, Piera. *Lonely Planet Hong Kong* (*Travel Guide*). Melbourne/Franklin, Tennessee/London/Beijing/Delhi: Lonely Planet, 2015.

Brown, Jules, and David Leffman. *Rough Guide to Hong Kong and Macau*. London: Rough Guides, 2009.

Scott Rutherford (ed.) *Hong Kong Insight Guide*. Hong Kong: Insight Guides, 2003.

Art and Architecture

Morris, Jan. *Building Hong Kong*. Hong Kong: FormAsia, 1995.

Moss, Peter. *Hong Kong style*. Hong Kong: FormAsia, 2000.

Politics and History

Fenby Jonathan. *Dealing with the Dragon. A Year in the New Hong Kong*. New York: Arcade Publishing, 2001.

Snow, Philip. *The Fall of Hong Kong: Britain, China and the Japanese Occupation*. Yale University Press, 2004.

Morris, Jan. *Hong Kong: Epilogue to an Empire*. London: Penguin Books, 1989.

Pullinger, Jackie, and Andrew Quicke. *Chasing the Dragon*. Hong Kong: Servant Ministries, reprinted 2004.

Moss, Peter. *Hong Kong Handover: Signed, Sealed & Delivered*. Hong Kong: FormAsia, 1999.

Cameron, Nigel, et al. *The Hong Kong Collection: Memorabilia of a Colonial Era*. Hong Kong: FormAsia, 1999.

Loh, Christine (Ed.). *Building Democracy: Creating Good Government for Hong Kong* (Civic Exchange Guides). Hong Kong: Hong Kong University Press, 2003.

Business

Lethbridge, David G. (Ed.), et al. *The Business Environment in Hong Kong*. Hong Kong: Oxford University Press (China), 2000

Shopping

Gershman, Suzy. *Born to Shop / Hong Kong, Shanghai & Beijing*. Hoboken, New Jersey: Wiley Publishing, Inc., 2010.

culture smart! **hong kong**

Index